forget to savor in our own lives as wives and mothers. Our children make our lives worth living. And worth writing about—if you can write like Danielle."

MAGGIE GALLAGHER

Coauthor of *The Case for Marriage* and president of the Institute for Marriage and Public Policy

"I read Danielle Bean's new book, *Mom to Mom, Day to Day*, while in the hospital after the birth of my eighth child. It was like having a chat over a backyard fence with an experienced mother who exudes an infectious joy. Danielle believes in vocation and loves the life to which God has called her. I wanted to jump up and give a copy to every new mother in the Birth Center that day!"

ELIZABETH FOSS

Author of *Real Learning, Education in the Heart of the Home*

D1169205

Mom to Mom,

DAY TO DAY

Mom to Mom,

DAY TO DAY

Advice and Support
for Catholic Living

By Danielle Bean

Pauline
BOOKS & MEDIA
Boston

Library of Congress Cataloging-in-Publication Data

Bean, Danielle.

  Mom to mom, day to day: advice and support for Catholic living /
by Danielle Bean.

       p. cm.

  Includes bibliographical references.

  ISBN 0-8198-4855-7 (pbk.)

  1. Motherhood—Religious aspects—Catholic Church. 2.
Mothers—Religious life. 3. Catholic women—Religious life. I. Title.

  BX2353.B42 2007

  248.8'431088282—dc22

                              2006028001

The Scripture quotations contained herein are from the *New Revised Standard Version Bible: Catholic Edition,* copyright © 1989, 1993, Division of Christian Education of the National Council of the Churches of Christ in the United States of America. Used by permission. All rights reserved.

Cover design by Rosana Usselmann

Cover photo: Image Source

Interior photos: pp. 1, 31: 2007 www.photospin.com
                 pp. 57, 77, 101, 129, Mary Emmanuel Alves, FSP

Published by Pauline Books & Media, 50 Saint Paul's Avenue, Boston, MA 02130-3491. www.pauline.org.

Printed in U.S.A.

Pauline Books & Media is the publishing house of the Daughters of St. Paul, an international congregation of women religious serving the Church with the communications media.

1 2 3 4 5 6 7 8 9   11 10 09 08 07

To my mother Marie,
and to my sisters Hélène, Suzanne, and Christine:
the women in my life who have taught me
the value of motherly sharing and
who have been there for me whenever I needed it.
I love you and I thank God for you.

Contents

one

How Can I Survive the Preschool Years Without Losing My Mind?

two

How Can I Fill My Marriage with More of "The Better" and Less of "The Worse"?

three

What Kind of Role Does a Catholic Mom Play in This Great Big World?

four

How Can I Get on Top of the Housework When It Feels Like I'm Smothering Under It?

five

How Can I Make Our Faith
an Integral Part of Family Life?

six

Can I Really Have a Spiritual Life
While Caring for All These Little People?

Preface

L et me begin by telling you that I'm not an expert. I'm an everyday mom—a fulltime wife and mother of eight, and a part-time writer. As a writer, I have maintained a blog at my Web site www.DanielleBean.com since 2004. Over time, as a result of my public discussion of issues ranging from husbands and housework to potties and pacifiers, many readers have been inspired to send me questions seeking advice and encouragement in their vocations as Catholic wives and mothers.

Though I'm not an authority in Catholic motherhood, this much I do know: Women stand to gain much from sharing their experiences, trials, and failings. When we gather together and seek advice from one another, we all benefit. Some of the wisest, most valuable advice I have ever received has been from my mother, my sisters, and my friends during long phone calls or e-mail conversations in which we commiserate, vent our frustrations, and objectively assess each other's personal struggles.

So when readers of my Web site began to send me questions, I recognized that they were turning to me as they would turn to a trusted friend. I've endeavored to respect that trust by answering their questions with a spirit of solidarity.

Though eventually I felt compelled to address some of the most frequently asked questions in the form of a book, I began this project with some trepidation. In my mind, there's something uncomfortably presumptuous about telling other people what to do. Many of us feel that anyone who dares to offer advice on any particular subject had best be a true authority on that subject. And by that I mean *perfect*.

I've read many motherly advice books where the authors have ultimately irritated me. Perhaps you've had similar experiences.

Who does this woman think she is? I find myself furiously thinking as I flip to the back cover to read the author's bio. *Is her family really so perfect? Doesn't her husband ever leave his balled-up, smelly socks on the bedroom floor and she snaps at him about it? Don't her kids ever argue about who's looking at whom, or who got the last cookie last time and who got it the time before that and who absolutely should not get it this time because he behaved so poorly when the babysitter was here last night? Doesn't she ever get just plain sick and tired of everyone in the world expecting her to have it all together all of the time? Doesn't she ever roll her eyes and hold back a sudden surge of nausea when someone suggests that the solution to all her personal problems is simply finding more time in her life for daily prayer?*

Well, dear friends, I'm going to anticipate your frustrated questions and head you off at the pass. My answer to all of the above is an incontrovertible YES. Those things absolutely happen to me. On some days, many times over. I am an imperfect woman married to an imperfect man and together we have brought into the world eight imperfect children. I'll even throw in the scandalous confessions that I don't iron, I pretty much never scrub out the oven, and, under the proper circumstances, I can be the queen of cynical sarcasm. Just ask that imperfect husband of mine.

I realize, though, that in our weaker moments, sometimes all we need is a sympathetic ear. We want someone to say, "I know how you feel," and really mean it. We want someone who has really been there to offer, "Here's what I did when that happened to me."

Addressing topics based on questions that have appeared on my Web site and new ones readers have sent me especially for this project, I hope to offer that kind of unpretentious encouragement here in these pages. The topics I tackle here are based on real concerns shared with me by real Catholic mothers from a wide variety of backgrounds and lifestyles.

The vocation of marriage and motherhood is fraught with complications and challenges. As God intends it to be our path to heaven, the living out of this vocation is likely to be the most difficult and yet the most fulfilling work any of us ever do. As you struggle and strain, rejoice and delight in the daunting occupation God has given to you, I hope that in this book you will find an ally—someone who truly "gets it" and who offers to share her thoughts with you. Sister to sister. Friend to friend. Mom to mom.

one

How Can I Survive the Preschool Years Without Losing My Mind?

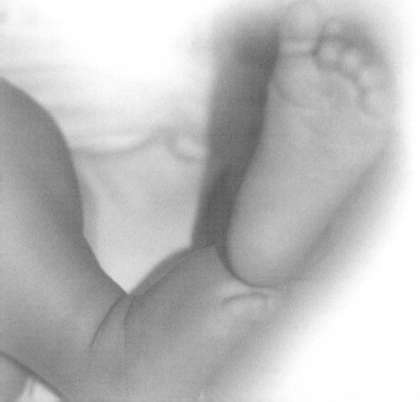

Saintly, or Just Plain Nuts?

When I was a new mother over eleven years ago, I gazed into my swaddled newborn daughter's eyes and was overcome with joy. And fear. When we brought her home from the hospital, I was overwhelmed with love. And exhaustion. The months that followed her birth were filled with bliss. And anxiety.

As trying and as frightening as the transition to motherhood was, it eventually made me a better person. I can see that now. When I was struggling my way through the battles of infancy and toddlerhood for the first time, though, I saw nothing but the struggle. I marveled at people who had many children, and that's why I have to laugh now when others marvel at me.

I was in the grocery store one day not too long ago when a woman behind me in line struck up a friendly conversation. Piles of groceries and three very active little boys were spilling from her cart. When she found out I was expecting my eighth child, she was incredulous.

"How do you do it?" she wanted to know.

"Oh, well, one day at a time, I suppose," I told her casually.

But she wasn't satisfied. "No, really," she pressed me. "*How do you do it?*"

She wanted a substantive explanation from a woman who appeared to be accomplishing the impossible. This young mother wanted real answers. And don't we all?

I often hear the "How do you do it?" question from disillusioned mothers of small children. They might once have dreamed of having a large family, but now, as they drown in diapers and tantrums, they begin to doubt their ability to handle any more than the two children they have. I meet them at the grocery store, the library, and in the church parking lot. To them, mothers of large families are superheroes. These are women of various ages and different backgrounds, but most of them have just one question: How on earth do you do it?

Well, I know you won't believe me, but here's my answer anyway: Having eight kids is easier than having one or two little ones. I should know. I once had just two children and, though I loved them dearly, I wouldn't in a million years trade the life I live now for the one I lived back then. My life with those two tiny people *was* overwhelming. Back then, when I met women with more children, I figured they must be either saintly or just plain nuts.

I suppose part of the reason life feels easier now is that I've been sufficiently "broken in." It's taken me a few years, but now I know that sometimes a baby is just going to cry, no matter what you do, and it doesn't mean you're a bad mother. I've also learned that bad haircuts grow out, potty training *does* eventually happen, and most things really do come out in the wash.

The biggest surprise, however, is that it's the kids themselves who make my life easier. Take yesterday afternoon, for example. When I had just two little babies, going to the store was an exhausting nightmare of buckling car seats, lugging babies through stores, and struggling to carry groceries into the house while keeping everyone content.

It's taken me a few years, but now I know that sometimes a baby is just going to cry, and it doesn't mean you're a bad mother.

Yesterday, however, when I piled all my kids into the van and took them out to run errands, it was quite a different experience. The older kids helped to buckle everyone in and then they held the younger ones' hands in parking lots and told them, "No running or shouting in the store, OK?" When we arrived home, everyone unbuckled, I handed the house keys to my oldest son, and everyone—right down to the three-year-old—carried in the diaper bag and the groceries. All I had to do was waltz into the opened house with the baby in my arms. Even the dog was let out and fed before I had taken off my coat.

Of course, my life doesn't always run so smoothly, but I can honestly say that I'm a more peaceful, happier person with many children than I was with just two. Remember this: God does not call the equipped; he equips the called. In my experience, God sent the babies first and then followed up with the graces as necessary. God gives us "our daily bread," the grace we need to live up to our responsibilities one day at a time. You don't have to have it all figured out and feel ready to handle a gang of kids years ahead of time. If God calls you to have a large family, he will help you to do it...one child at a time.

It's the Little Things

I don't know about you, but I can handle big disasters. I actually keep my cool rather well in crisis situations. It's the little things that get me. Some days, the continual accumulation of tiny annoyances builds and builds until at great long last it threatens to do me in.

One recent Saturday, my husband, Dan, took the older boys fishing. Left alone with the other children for the afternoon, I decided we could get a start on some gardening work that needed to be done. The strawberry patch was most pressing—the plants had arrived a few days before and had been weighing on my conscience ever since. The box was well stamped with warnings: PERISHABLE PRODUCT! PLANT IMMEDIATELY! DO NOT DELAY!

But we had nowhere ready to plant them yet. So I put baby Raphael down for his nap and asked Kateri to find me a shovel. Raphael must have sensed my impending plans for actually accomplishing something. He whined. He shouted. He sobbed. But he would not nap.

Well, it was a beautiful, sunny afternoon, so I scooped him from his bed, brought him outside, and plunked him—

barefoot—in the sandbox. I charged Juliette with supervising him, picked up the shovel, and headed into the field.

As it turned out, however, the grassy spot I had scouted out for the strawberries was actually a rather mossy spot. Thickly mossy. Densely mossy. Though I stabbed at the earth with the shovel, it remained obstinate. At one point, I managed to get the blade of the shovel to break through just a bit, and then I proceeded to jump on it with both feet. This acrobatic performance did little to improve the situation.

For her part, three-year-old Gabrielle was doing little to improve the situation either. She parked herself on the ground beside me and moaned about a recent injury. If I held my head to one side and squinted at her knee just so, I could barely make out a tiny, almost-pink line where she had suffered a scrape after falling off her tricycle.

"Need band-aid, Mama," she whined. "Neeeeeeeeeeeed band-aaaaaaaaaaaaaid."

It was right about that time that the beautiful springtime sun became vicious. It mercilessly beat down upon my back and shoulders, and I felt a trickle of sweat form between my shoulder blades.

It was right about that time, too, that the black flies made their appearance. Where on earth did they come from? And how could I have not noticed them before? They swarmed and buzzed in my ears. Perniciously, they bit at my neck and weaseled their way into my eyes, my nostrils, and down my shirt.

Come to think of it, it was right about that time, too, that Raphael tired of the sandbox and called for me, arms outstretched, from across the field. It was right about then that I knelt down on the ground to examine it and felt the cold wet of recent rains seep through the knees of my jeans. It was right about then that I realized I had been attempting to overturn not a small patch of earth but an enormous, moss-covered chunk of granite. It was right about then that I recalled that the strawberry patch was my husband's idea in the first place. It was right about then that I remembered I had left a load of clothes in the dryer that were probably sitting, cold and wrinkled, awaiting my attention in the house. It was right about then that I thought of the casserole I had intended to put together during Raphael's nap and the chicken I had neglected to remove from the freezer that morning.

I will spare you (okay, me) the details of what happened next. Maybe some wildly immature person threw a shovel and shouted out something she shouldn't have. Anyway, it's none of your business if she did. She probably doesn't usually do that kind of thing and maybe she felt bad about it afterwards and it was probably just all those little annoying things that got to her.

Because motherhood can be so overwhelming and because all the necessary, tiny tasks that make up our daily routines as wives and mothers can be so mind-numbing and frustrating, I'm in good company. Many mothers I know struggle with controlling their tempers.

Sometimes, even perfect strangers will ask me: "Do you ever have a bad day? Do you ever yell at your kids?" Every time, I can hear the hope and uncertainty in the questioners' voices. They want desperately to know: Is this normal? Am I a bad mother because I lose my temper sometimes? Do other mothers yell at their kids?

Why, oh why, do we women insist upon torturing ourselves with the thought that every mother in the world is perfect...except ourselves?

Why, oh why, do we women insist upon torturing ourselves with the thought that every mother in the world is perfect...except ourselves?

When we see a cheerful woman with well-behaved children in the grocery store or at Mass, why do we assume she never has a bad moment? Why do we think that other moms have it all together all the time? Why do we imagine that other women have perfect marriages, ever-orderly homes, and sophisticated spiritual lives? Why do we believe that we are the only ones who ever get tired or cranky or just plain "sick of it" and yell at our children?

We all have different temperaments, of course, so some mothers are going to struggle with their tempers more than others. But I really do believe that every mother does yell at her kids, at least occasionally. As a natural consequence of embracing the motherly vocation, we will have our patience tried and tried and tried. This is part of the difficulty of parenting that might not be immediately apparent to an outside observer. The spilled juice. The whiny two-year-old. The bickering preteens. The dishes, the laundry, the carpooling. Eventually, some small thing happens, like a potty mess or an act of disobedience, and we lose it. We yell. We might even cry. And then we feel terrible afterward.

Reactions and Overreactions

Do good mothers ever yell at their kids? As is probably painfully obvious in the example I have shared above, this mother surely does. Sometimes when they deserve it and sometimes when they don't. Over the years, however, I find that I have become less of a "yeller." This has little to do with motherly perfection and more to do with the fact that over time I've found that yelling at kids is not all that effective. Besides, it sounds and feels terrible.

I think that my reactions (and overreactions) to everyday challenges and my children's behavior have changed over the years as a natural consequence of a combination of things.

First, because I have a gang of kids now instead of just one or two, I've had to learn to relax a bit. With the passing of time and the growth of our family, I've discovered the importance of letting go of things that don't really matter in the long run. I choose instead to focus on those behaviors I really want to encourage or discourage in my kids. There's a lot of truth in that old advice to "pick your battles." It makes for less conflict and less frustration. Some behaviors are just irritating or minor infractions that don't require parental intervention every time they happen. If a parent responds to every little thing her children do every minute of the day, a blowup becomes inevitable. No one can keep that up for very long.

What's more, if you yell all the time, your family learns to tune you out. As a mother of preschoolers, it dawned on me one day that I was doing an awful lot of yelling because it was the only way I could get anyone to listen to me. The kids had learned to tune out my calm, quiet requests and instructions because they knew that eventually, if I really meant it, I would yell. They waited for that to happen before they would bother to respond.

Fixing this problem meant I had to give up lazy parenting. A real bummer, I know. Here's how non-lazy parenting works: You need to teach your children that you mean what you say the first time you say it. If you say, "Please stop throwing that ball in the house," and get no response, you have to set aside the potatoes you are peeling for dinner, physically remove the ball, and find an appropriate consequence for the offender.

It's a pain, I know. Screaming at the kid while you continue to peel the potatoes might be easier, but it sets a poor example and is ineffective in the long run. Breaking bad habits requires conscious effort but results in real benefits if we make the effort. If we follow through on our commands with appropriate punishments every time, it doesn't take children long to figure out that mom means what she says—the first time—and that it's in their best interest to respond to that first request.

All of this said, I really want to emphasize the fact that no one is perfect. Every mom loses patience and raises her voice now and then, sometimes unfairly. If nothing else, I hope that anxious moms will understand this: Messing up sometimes and losing your temper doesn't mean you are a bad mother. It means you are human. Apologize, pray for the strength to respond more lovingly the next time, and then get back to peeling the potatoes.

Toddler Eruptions

Parents aren't the only ones who struggle with controlling anger and frustration. Nothing brings out a parent's temper quite like an unreasonable child's temper tantrum. Ultimately, how we express our own anger and frustration, though, speaks volumes to our children, who are watching our every move and preparing to imitate our behavior. Some of the most trying years are when a child is between the ages of two and four. These little humans can be the most willful little creatures on the planet. In my experience, especially when a toddler is in the process of giving up afternoon naps, the dinner hour can produce some pretty awful flare-ups.

During these most trying of moments, it's quite likely that you and your husband do not always respond as lovingly and patiently as you know you should. We all have our less-than-shining parental moments. One important thing is for the two of you to decide ahead of time how you'll deal with a child's uncontrolled tantrums. While one of you is holding a screeching, arching, kicking kid is no time to be attempting to discuss your parental approach. Find a calm, quiet moment and talk about it then so that you can present a unified front when the inevitable happens. Decide together in what specific ways you will handle tantrum behavior. Clarify that name-calling or out-of-control screaming at small children is unacceptable. Decide too how you intend to handle tantrums in public places, because—guess what?— they're going to happen.

My personal preference for dealing with toddler tantrums is to put the child in a safe place and calmly tell her (my current tantrum child is a "her") that she can come out when she's not screaming or crying. But then, of course, you have to be prepared to enforce the rule. Sometimes I have to return my little darling to her room ten times before she's done, each time repeating that she can come out when she's ready to be reasonable. Eventually, she does calm down and I let her come out and join the family again. If there was any serious misbehavior, I sit her down and we talk about it calmly before she can play. Naturally, we always end up with reassuring hugs and kisses! This approach teaches her that tantrum-type behavior will not be tolerated, but that we love her and welcome her presence—when she's ready to behave appropriately.

Dealing with toddler behavior is enormously challenging for every parent. Some days we handle it better than other days. What I've described here is an ideal approach, but it surely is not one that I manage to practice every single time a toddler erupts in a tantrum. For the sake of your own sanity, keep in mind that even with the best-laid plan, no parent is going to maintain a perfect disciplinary track record. But fear not. One less-than-perfect parental moment is not going to permanently scar your child. On the whole, your loving, consistent management of misbehavior will pay off with a close and mutually respectful relationship in the long run.

Surviving Church

Sometimes, Mass goes swimmingly. But other times…I tell Stephen to stop humming. I try not to notice that Gabrielle dropped her pacifier on the gritty floor and then popped it back into her mouth before I could intervene. I tell Stephen to stop biting the hymnal. I realize that my lap is wet and that Gabrielle needs a diaper change—coincidentally, at the exact same moment. I tell Stephen to stop poking his brother. I struggle to maintain my dignity as Raphael stuffs a fistful of my hair in his mouth, gags, and then spits up on my sweater. I tell Stephen to stop lifting the kneeler. I whisper to Gabrielle that Jesus is on the altar and she corrects me loudly: "No, *dat* Jesus!" while pointing at the statue of the Sacred Heart. I tell Stephen to stop undressing the baby. And finally, when I hear Father say, "The Mass is ended. Go in peace," no one responds with greater enthusiasm than I: "Thanks be to God! Alleluia!"

I will not try to convince you that taking little kids to Mass is easy, because it isn't. And I am not going to tell you that I know some magic formula and my kids are always perfectly behaved at Mass, because I don't and they aren't. I am going to tell you, however, that bringing small children to Mass *is* worth doing.

I think bringing books along to Mass (especially a child's missal) can be a good idea, but I really recommend limiting the number of "toys" you might be tempted to bring. Doing "fun activities" during Mass, like coloring or playing with trucks, can give children the wrong idea about why we go to church. Besides, these can be distracting to older kids, or even to grown-ups, in the pews around you.

Children are more capable of a sense of reverence than we realize.

Children are more capable of a sense of reverence than we realize. They won't learn proper behavior in church if we never take them. And they won't learn proper behavior in church if we take them but give them an unspoken message of: Sit and play here for an hour while we grown-ups have our Mass and keep telling you to be quiet. They just might begin to get the right idea, though, if we help them to pray. If we include them. If we tell them: "This is God's house. Jesus is here in the tabernacle. We receive Jesus in Communion. We came here to be with God and tell him how much we love him."

Kids are naturally noisy and active with short attention spans, so we have to be reasonable in our expectations. You have to understand ahead of time that there are going to be times when your kids fuss and cry and you have to leave the pew. If this makes you uncomfortable,

sit in the back, where you're less likely to be a disturbance. In my own experience, however, kids do better sitting up near the front so that they can see everything that
is going on and feel a part of the Mass.

Whatever you decide, though, don't let the fact that
you have small children prevent you from going to Mass.
You belong there and they are welcome too. Our Lord
himself invited them: "Let the little children come to me;
do not stop them; for it is to such as these that the king-
dom of God belongs" (Mk 10:14).

Who are we to disagree?

Do What Works Best for Your Family

Through the years I've read many parenting books and found much helpful wisdom in many of them, "attachment parenting" books included. My reading and experience, however, have led me to the conclusion that parenting philosophies are dangerous things.

In the end, I've rejected all the expert parenting philosophies. This isn't because there's anything particularly bad about any of them. Experience has simply led me to employ a different parenting philosophy in their place: my own. I call mine *Do What Works Best for Your Family*.

I find it amusing that there are so many different parenting "experts" out there who don't hesitate to tell other parents that their particular philosophy is the one right way to raise children, or at least imply it. It's not just attachment parenting proponents, either. In some groups with which I've been associated, parenting philosophy feels almost like a pseudo-religion. The implication is that following a particular set of rules will make you a good mother. In fact, they imply it so effectively that many mothers (and I have been one of them) suffer from feelings of guilt and failure when things don't go as smoothly as the books tell them they should.

Well, I already have a religion, thank you.

There are so many wonderfully different kinds of families with different circumstances. There are so many wonderfully different kinds of children with different temperaments and needs. There are so many wonderfully different kinds of mothers with different personalities, strengths, and weaknesses. For some women, baby-wearing and co-sleeping feel marvelously natural. Others might struggle with backaches and sleep problems that make them miserable human beings if they try to be "perfectly attached."

You are the number one expert on the best approach for your family at any given time.

Do What Works Best for Your Family. That might mean exclusively breastfeeding, or not. It might mean using a pacifier and an infant swing. You know yourself and your children better than any author of any book ever could. You are the number one expert on the best approach for your family at any given time. Use that expertise.

I've been employing the *Do What Works Best for Your Family* philosophy for many happy, guilt-free years now. In fact, as I have watched my babies throughout the years, this much is apparent: Babies don't care what we call it. They know when they are loved and cared for.

They know when their mothers are relaxed and happy. So when presented with a parental challenge, go ahead and read the books, talk to the experts, and survey your playgroup. In the end, however, take and use only what works best for you and your family. Toss the rest…and the guilt along with it.

Nighttime Visitors

L ack of regular sleep is one of the number one complaints you will hear from parents of young children. It sure would be nice sometimes to "clock out," but it certainly is true that parenting is a twenty-four-hour-a-day occupation. Particularly during the preschool years, many parents are frustrated by a child's inability or unwillingness to sleep through the night on his own.

Some parenting experts recommend that the problem of wakeful children can be resolved simply by inviting the children into your bed. Well, this particular solution has never worked for me. I think that parents who are disturbed by a child coming to their room at night have already tried and rejected the idea of the "family bed." They are not looking for a family bed. The family bed doesn't work for them, and *that's* the problem.

Personally, I cannot bear to spend all night in the same bed with a child after he or she is about six months old. I love my children every bit as much as co-sleeping moms love theirs, but once they kick and squirm and sprawl, the party's over. And it's not just about me, either. My husband finds it impossible to get proper rest when there is a largish, mobile third party in the bed, and I find that after a certain age my children tend to sleep better on their own as well.

So, if the "family bed" is not the solution and your children still insist upon coming into your bedroom, how *can* your family get the rest it needs?

It's been my experience that nighttime wakefulness can be a passing phase in a child's life. Perhaps during stressful times or when family changes are taking place, an older child sometimes develops a very real need for extra attention and parental security. One solution that has worked well for us in these kinds of situations is to set up a child's sleeping area in the parents' bedroom. A spare crib mattress on the floor works well. Even a "bed" made up of floor pillows and blankets that are placed near the parents' bed offers a cozy, near-to-Mom-and-Dad sleeping location for a needy child.

Many of our children have gone through phases of getting up at night, but I've found that by using this system, we minimize the disturbance they cause. Some children do become middle-of-the-night "regulars" on the floor in our room for a little while. More often than not, though, they slip in unnoticed and settle into the pre-made, child-sized bed on the floor all on their own.

We've found that if we remain casual and accommodating about their nighttime need for closeness, as they grow older, they eventually outgrow the wakefulness. For example, between the ages of four and five, our daughter Juliette was one of our most frequent nighttime visitors.

Today, at six years old, she sleeps quite contentedly on her own. Sometimes, in the morning, I look at the small, empty bed beside our own and feel a pang of longing for the tiny girl who once needed this spot so close to her mother's side. But then I have to smile at the happy milestone our closeness and support has enabled our daughter to achieve. Secure, satisfied children and relaxed, rested parents make for a happy household indeed!

Unexpectedly Expecting

Sometimes God's plans for our lives don't match our own. Never is this made more abundantly clear to a woman than when she finds herself unexpectedly pregnant. I have had this experience myself, and know all too well the storm of conflicted emotions that accompany an unplanned pregnancy.

Beneath the fluorescent lights in the bathroom of the tiny apartment Dan and I shared as newlyweds years ago, two clear pink lines were unmistakable. I was pregnant. Newly graduated from college and newly married, I was pregnant. With a husband who was a full-time student, with no job, and with no health insurance, I was pregnant. Faced with this unexpected news, I did what any mature woman does when things don't go exactly the way she has planned: I sat on the floor and I cried.

As a pro-life activist and a cradle Catholic, I immediately recognized the tiny life within me as a unique and infinitely precious person. That wasn't the problem. Objectively, I knew I could welcome the new life as a gift from God, but I still couldn't escape a feeling of extreme disappointment. Having a baby so soon would disrupt the plans we had made for the first year of our marriage. Dan was supposed to complete his master's degree and find a secure job as a teacher before we had children. I was supposed to find a full-time job with benefits to support us while he finished his coursework. Instead, here I was—a straight-A student who had failed her first real-life test in Natural Family Planning.

In the following weeks, as I battled nausea and exhaustion while waiting tables at a seafood restaurant, I wallowed in self-pity. And the worst part was that I was overcome with guilt for feeling so negative about something that my heart told me should be a happy event. Despite my pessimism, things worked out well for us.

An unplanned pregnancy always brings a roller-coaster ride of emotions.

I didn't fully realize the perfection of God's plan until nine months later, though, when I gave birth to the most beautiful and charming child anyone had ever laid eyes upon. Finally, I understood: God sent us this child because *she* was meant to be ours—not one that we might have conceived in another year or two. Dan and I needed Kateri and, in his goodness, God made sure that we got her—in spite of our plans.

The happy ending, however, doesn't negate the difficult feelings I had in accepting my pregnancy in the first place. An unplanned pregnancy always brings a roller-coaster ride of emotions. And it might not be your first pregnancy that catches you by surprise, but one that occurs when you already have a houseful of children to handle. It can be easy to feel somewhat less than thrilled to find out that the stork will be visiting your house yet again. And easy, too, to feel guilty for your initial lack of joy.

It really is normal to balk a bit at unanticipated, life-altering news. Even if we recognize each tiny new life as an irreplaceable gift from God, that knowledge alone doesn't prevent the very human reaction of sometimes recoiling at the thought of taking on a new pregnancy. Pregnancy and eventually a new baby can bring stress, work, little sleep, restricted freedom, and little rest in between.

Giving voice to the thoughts and fears that come with an unexpected pregnancy shouldn't cause anyone to feel guilty. Christ himself suffered fear and dread the night before his crucifixion—not because he would have any other than God's will be done, but simply because he knew the cross that lay ahead. And he dreaded the pain.

We humans cling to the false notion that ultimately *we* are in control of our lives. Finding ourselves unexpectedly pregnant reminds us of the uncomfortable truth: We are not in charge. Sometimes the hardest words in the world to pray and to really mean are "Thy will be done." We fear that God's will might not match our own. We forget that when God sends us a new challenge, he also sends us the graces we need to handle it.

Not long ago, I found myself standing in my bathroom repeating a familiar scene as I stared at two unmistakable pink lines. My mind raced. Another baby? Could I start the new school year with debilitating morning sickness?

Could we handle a new baby at a time of year when Dan's work schedule becomes more demanding? Would the addition to our house be completed before the baby was born or would we find ourselves still more cramped for space? Was our family *really* ready for another child?

Even as these anxious questions sped through my mind, though, I could feel myself beginning to smile an inward smile. Experience has taught me this much: God gave due consideration to my concerns way back when he planned to give us this new little person to love. Is our family ready to welcome another child? God answered that question ages ago. He said yes.

❧

Dear Lord, thank you for making me a mother. I love these little souls you have entrusted to my care. I love their unconditional love, their ready forgiveness, their sweetness, their innocence. Help me to remember the unique and infinite value of each of my children, even when they overwhelm me. Even when they frustrate me. Even when they try my patience in a thousand different ways. In moments of anxiety and weakness, remind me always to turn to you. Give me peace and strength that can only come from you. Bathe my humble efforts in your Precious Blood and make me a worthy mother to these children here on earth. Guide all of us to know, love, and serve you better so that we may one day all live together with you in heaven. Amen.

two

How Can I Fill My Marriage with More of "The Better" and Less of "The Worse"?

Splitting Housework, Splitting Hairs

Years ago, a faraway friend of mine called me in tears. Her marriage, she managed to tell me between sobs and sniffles, was in trouble. She never thought she would be one of "those people" who experiences marital troubles, but here she was, and she didn't know what to do.

So what was the problem? Infidelity? Abuse? Mental illness?

Well, no. As it turned out, all of their marital strife centered around...the kitchen garbage can.

You see, it was *his* turn out take out the trash. And just like every other time when it was his turn, the trash was piling up. It was spilling over onto the kitchen tiles. She was having trouble keeping the baby from playing in it. And despite her best efforts at nagging and reminding, griping and complaining, my friend's husband remained obstinate. He was tired, he told her. He was busy. He was *not* going to take out the trash. That morning, after hours of posturing and wrangling, the two of them had finally exploded in an enormous argument over the stupid garbage can. They both said things they shouldn't have, and then he left the house in a fit of anger.

I tried to reassure my friend that her marriage was not, in fact, over. I told her I was sure her husband would return, and then I encouraged her to take out the trash herself, as a sign of her willingness to make peace when he did come home. But her response surprised me.

"But if *I* take out the trash," she protested, "*he* wins."

Keeping Score

As childish and silly as her words sounded to me at the time, I had to admit that the competitive, controlling sentiment behind them sounded familiar. When I was first married and particularly when I became a mother, the splitting of household work was an issue that I struggled with a great deal. Despite my best efforts, I seemed unable to rid myself of the "feminist" thinking that saturates our culture on this topic. Although in many ways I loved my role as a wife and mother, all too often my underlying assumption was that preparing meals, cleaning up, and baby care were servile work and there was no reason in the world that I should be the one stuck doing it all. I kept mental track of who did which chores and whose "turn" it was this time. If I did some extra task that I considered my husband's job, I kept a mental score of that, too. If I saw my husband relaxing when there was still work to do, I made a mental note of that as well. *I* was on duty twenty-four hours a day. *I* never got a break like that. Hmmmmph.

Some women might not like what I have to say here, but because it has helped me in marriage so much, I'm going to just grit my teeth and say it. I think that modern so-called feminist thinking has done a great deal of damage to marriage by creating the expectation of a 50/50 sharing of household and childcare duties, particularly in families where one spouse stays home and the other spouse works full time.

> *This much I have learned: If you keep score, everybody loses.*

This much I have learned: If you keep score, everybody loses. The constant worrying and arguing about who does what, who did it last time, and who does more is not only unpleasant—it's exhausting. And it makes everyone miserable. What ever happened to giving without counting the cost?

When I think about it clearly and am honest with myself, I have to admit that my husband's outside work is every bit as servile as the work I do around the house. Does he get up at the crack of dawn, scrape the ice from his windshield, and slog his way into work every morning because it's glamorous and he enjoys it? Of course not. He does it because he loves his family and intends to *serve* us by providing for our material needs. I might scrub the toilet more often than my husband does but, on the other hand, I have the luxury of making my own daily schedule and enjoying unexpected breaks during my day.

I can clearly recall the summer I spent pregnant with our third child. Every day, I let the kids play in their outdoor kiddie pool until they had exhausted themselves. After that, we headed inside for changes and naptime.

For *everyone*. That summer, I pulled the shades and enjoyed a two-to-three-hour nap in the cool of an electric fan every single day while my husband worked his sweltering summer job landscaping a golf course.

It was right about that time that I had to admit that my mental chore war didn't make much sense. I made a bold decision to take on all of the household jobs. They became mine. Entirely. I stopped nagging and I stopped expecting any kind of routine household contribution from my husband beyond repair work, trips to the dump, and other traditionally "male" tasks that he had always been very good about keeping up with anyway. I let go of the interior anger and resentment that made no sense.

And guess what? It worked. Well, maybe not always perfectly, but it made a decided difference in my mental well-being and in our relationship. Before you go getting any crazy ideas, however, please know that my husband is not a chauvinistic slob and I am not Super Woman. Dan happens to have a work schedule that allows him to be home during daytime hours on a regular basis. This has proved most helpful to our balance of responsibilities. He is able to take on a significant portion of homeschooling duties during the day in order to free me up for attending to the little ones, catching up on laundry, or even— ahem—writing a book.

Still, though, I'm only one human being with a limited amount of time and energy, so I can't always complete all the household work I assign to myself. Something I have discovered, however, is that when chores are less of a tug-of-war between the two of us, my husband is more inclined to help out even when I don't ask him to. Instead of being a hen-pecked husband who is bullied into doing his "fair share," he gets to be a helpful hero to his appreciative wife.

Ultimately, I find that splitting housework, like most other parts of marriage, works out best when both spouses worry less about fairness to themselves and consider the other person's needs first. My work in the home serves my husband and makes his life easier and more pleasant—he appreciates that. And his work outside the home provides for our family's material needs and enables me to stay home with the children—I appreciate that. It's not a bad deal for either of us, really.

Of course I don't expect that the exact solution to the chore war that has worked in my marriage will work in exactly the same way for anyone else. All couples have different arrangements with regard to household duties, and these will vary according to personal preferences as well as who works outside the home and who doesn't. I just hope to encourage more women to drop the worries about what's fair and to stop keeping score when it comes to household contributions. Focus instead on all the non-housework ways your husband may serve the family and worry more about cultivating your own generous spirit. In the end, it's not just a favor to your husband, it's a favor to yourself. And to your marriage.

Asking and Receiving

N ow perhaps you're wondering: What about those times when you really do need help with housework, and yet your husband seems oblivious to your distress? Don't we all wish our husbands would just recognize our need for help and give it…without waiting to be asked? When we are struggling to get the kids ready for bed all by ourselves, we shouldn't have to ask him to turn off the television and pitch in, should we?

When we feel this kind of frustration, we need to ask ourselves: Do we really want our husbands' help or do we want them to read our minds?

Ultimately, whether or not you "have to" ask for help in these situations depends upon whether or not you really want your husband's help. Generally speaking, men are terrible mind readers. While women can be quite skilled at discerning the feelings and needs of others, we are too often unfair in our demand that the men in our lives demonstrate an equal capacity to do so. Most men will respond more positively to a direct request for help than to a sudden, inexplicable (to them), angry attitude from a resentful wife whose needs aren't being met.

So, when dinner is burning, the dog is chasing a naked two-year-old, and the older kids commence a spitting fight while our darling husbands sit obliviously in the midst of the chaos absorbed in a good book…should we *have* to say, "Would you mind catching Johnny and putting a diaper on him?"

Does it really matter? All I know is that if we really want the baby diapered, we probably *do* have to say it, and everyone will be happier in the end if we just do it. Forget your pride or how you think things should be and just ask, already. Nicely, of course. And be sure to give him positive feedback when he does help out.

Giving and Getting

B etween my husband and me, I'm usually the one who gets up with baby Raphael in the morning and changes his diaper. One recent morning, however, Dan got up before I did. He changed the baby and fed him before I was even out of bed. Raphael is a productive child, though, and by the time I got up, he had managed to fill his diaper again. As I set about getting a diaper and changing him, Dan happened into the room.

"Oh," he observed casually, "did he need to be changed *again?*"

I had to smile. I had noticed Dan's help with the baby but had neglected to mention it; my dear husband was just making sure I knew that this was the *second* diaper change of the day and that his contribution was recognized. After I thanked him profusely, we both laughed. Since that time, the incident has become a bit of an ongoing joke between us, and we both occasionally go to outrageous lengths in order to ensure that our efforts are recognized and appreciated.

The underlying issue, however, is a serious one. We all have a very real need to have our contributions valued and acknowledged. And even a little bit of praise goes a long way. I must confess, though, that even after I managed to let go of the 50/50 nonsense with regard to housework, I still sometimes struggled with the idea that my husband seemed to "expect a band to play" every time he put a glass in the sink. I found myself balking a bit at the "helpful hero" status he got to assume when he did housework while I had to slave away, alone and unappreciated, with only the dirty laundry to keep me company.

We all have a very real need to have our contributions valued and acknowledged.

"What about *me?*" I would sometimes think and at other times even dare to say out loud. "No one is thanking or appreciating me! I load the dishwasher in my sleep. I scrub the pots, I vacuum the rugs, I shake out the doormats, I set the table, I make the dinners, I change the diapers, I dust the furniture, I do the laundry, I do the shopping, I shake all the crumbs out of that tray thingy in the bottom of the toaster and then polish the chrome, but nobody calls me a hero for doing any of that!"

Before I get myself too worked up, though, I try to stop myself with the following question: Am I doing these things to serve God and my family or am I doing these things to gain admiration and appreciation?

In my experience, like it or not, most men do consider household tasks primarily female responsibilities. In his mind, therefore, when he loads the dishwasher, my husband is crossing a line—he is going above and beyond the call of duty, the same way I would feel if some winter day I decided to do him a favor and shovel the walkway before he got around to it. A man is going to expect immediate and positive feedback for making such a bold and daring move, more than he generally gets for his "regular" contributions to the household.

The good news is, however, that it doesn't have to kill me to give my husband the appreciation he seeks. No need to fall over in a faint. A simple "Wow, honey! Thanks for loading the dishwasher!" with a hug or kiss usually does the trick. And then I don't go rearranging everything in the dishwasher when he's through. I just try to focus on being genuinely grateful, and that's it.

Ultimately, I have come to realize, my husband wants to be my hero. If I can make him feel like a hero for loading the dishwasher, he might even be motivated enough to sweep the floor next time.

See? Everybody wins.

God's Choicest Blessings

B efore I attempt to address this topic, I want to begin with a big fat disclaimer: I am no kind of expert and I am not an authority on this subject. There are way too many people out there who pretend to know what is best for everyone and are more than eager to share their family-planning opinions with the world. Just think of the busybodies who insist on asking a couple who struggles with infertility, "When are the two of you going to ever have a baby?" And need I mention the reproductive police who patrol the aisles of your local supermarket? "What? Pregnant again? Don't you two own a television?"

No, sir. I stoutly refuse to join their ranks.

I will not pretend to know what is best for everyone because of course I don't. How on earth could I? Just as God does not have a single "correct" plan of life for all individuals, neither does he have a single "correct" blueprint for the perfect family size. But of course that's where the discernment comes in. And that's where so many of us have questions. We know that we're supposed to make responsible, moral decisions regarding the size of our families, but how exactly do we do that?

Well, let's see... How should serious Catholics approach making any important decision? We should begin with open hearts and minds. We should consult the teachings of the Church. We should seek spiritual direction if needed. And we should *pray*.

Church Teaching

In *Gaudium et Spes (Pastoral Constitution on the Church in the Modern World)*, the Second Vatican Council reminds us that: "Marriage and conjugal love are by their nature ordained toward the begetting and educating of children. Children are really the supreme gift of marriage and contribute very substantially to the welfare of their parents."

Then, in *Humanae Vitae (Of Human Life)*, Pope Paul VI further explains:

In relation to physical, economic, psychological and social conditions, responsible parenthood is exercised, either by the deliberate and generous decision to raise a numerous family, or by the decision, made for grave motives and with due respect for the moral law, to avoid for the time being, or even for an indeterminate period, a new birth.

He continues:

If, then, there are serious motives to space out births, which derive from the physical or psychological conditions of husband and wife, or from external conditions, the Church teaches that it is then licit to take into account the natural rhythms immanent in the generative functions, for the use of marriage in the infecund periods only, and in this way to regulate birth without offending the moral principles which have been recalled earlier.

So we learn that having children and raising them are the natural and primary purposes of marriage and sex. And it is further made clear that we are called to use only natural, moral means of regulating births and to do so only when we have "grave motives."

My guess is that most couples who struggle with discerning family size find the "grave motives" part the tricky part. What exactly qualifies as a "grave motive"? Well, if you ask around, you can find people who will tell you that nothing short of certain death or destitute poverty qualify as grave motives. And if you ask around some more, you can find people who will tell you that wanting to avoid stretch marks is a grave motive.

I won't tell you either of those things. What I will tell you is that *God* knows what qualifies as a grave motive for you and your family and that if you really are wondering what's best for you and your family, you need to ask *him*. That's where the next part comes in...

Prayer

I firmly believe that those who find themselves at odds with a spouse over whether or not to have another child, or those who question their real motives for wanting to have or wanting to postpone another pregnancy, can find resolution only through prayer.

If you honestly seek to know and to do God's will, all you need to do is ask him for help in doing so. He will not fail to answer you. Don't pray, however, that God will change your husband's mind and give you permission to have another baby. Don't pray either that God will open your husband's eyes to the financial necessity of avoiding another pregnancy.

Keep your heart open to hearing God's answer.

That's not honest and that's not open. Pray instead that both you and your spouse will come to know and accept God's will for your family. And then keep your heart open to hearing the answer, even if it's not the one you want to hear.

For those who use Natural Family Planning (see the Resource Guide beginning on page 151), deciding whether or not to have a baby is not a permanent decision but a month-by-month decision. And, as it turns out, in NFP there is a built-in motivator that encourages couples to be open to life and generous with their fertility: Abstinence is neither easy nor fun. Couples who use NFP to avoid pregnancy must ask themselves each month, "Are our reasons for avoiding pregnancy at this time serious enough to warrant this kind of personal sacrifice?" In this way, NFP encourages its users to discern family size thoughtfully, carefully, and generously.

Finally, whatever you decide, during your fertile years I would encourage you to keep open the question of having another child. There are enough couples out there gleefully announcing, "No more children for us! No way! Not ever!" We don't need to join the anti-life chorus.

For married couples, children are God's choicest blessings. May we always be mindful of the blessings of children and may God guide us in every decision we make for the betterment of our families.

Oh, and Happy Anniversary

I will never forget our first wedding anniversary. My husband made reservations for the three of us (by that time, we had a three-month-old daughter) at a gorgeous hotel in Vermont. In the evenings, while the baby slept, we relaxed in the Jacuzzi, toasted one another, and sipped champagne.

I'll never forget our tenth wedding anniversary, either. I was changing the baby's diaper (our sixth) when Dan breezed into the room. He hastily checked the calendar, told me he was late for an appointment at the eye doctor, and grabbed his car keys.

"Oh, and happy anniversary," he said, as he dashed out the door. I sat in silence for a moment, holding the baby and straining my brain to remember what the date was.

"Right. Happy anniversary," I said to no one in particular, as Dan's car backed out of the driveway.

After a few kids or a few years, even the most loving of marriages go through a period of romantic transition. Gone are the long leisurely walks in the moonlight, each of you gazing into the other's eyes, sharing your innermost thoughts and loving feelings. Somewhere along the way, the two of you tossed your rose-colored, heart-shaped glasses in favor of a horn-rimmed pair of more practical spectacles. Out with the surprise love notes, small romantic gifts, loving looks, and compliments...in with the colicky babies, mortgage payments, stomach flu, and car pools!

But you probably know that much already. You just want to know if you should accept the fact that romance is dead and get back to cleaning the bathroom. Well, I am here to tell you that all hope is not lost. You just might need to change your expectations a bit. The unfortunate fact is that what once came quite naturally now requires a bit of effort. But it *is* a worthwhile effort.

Let's begin by admitting that wives are not the only ones to mourn their dating days and the early days of marriage. I think that perhaps husbands just tend to miss different things about our more romantic times. In my experience, my husband tends to crave physical attention. Generally speaking, he feels most loved when I prepare him food the way he likes it, keep an orderly home, provide him with clean clothing, and provide him with physical affection.

I, on the other hand, tend to crave emotional attention. I feel most loved when Dan takes the time to ask about my feelings, to compliment my appearance, and to appreciate my contributions. I am not a complicated creature. I can last all day on a single "You look pretty today" and an extra kiss from my husband in the morning.

Ultimately, I think neither of us has complicated needs for love and attention. The problem, however, is that meeting one another's needs *does* require some conscious effort. As family life gets more demanding, that extra effort is all too easily dropped from our schedules.

Meeting one another's needs does *require some conscious effort.*

For example, when my life is busy, I can rather easily slide into the habit of focusing on my children's needs in the morning and "forgetting" that Dan likes a hot breakfast before work. And after a long day of caring for the children, any woman can feel quite justified in claiming she is too tired to respond to her husband's sexual advances.

Likewise, can I reasonably expect Dan to notice that I mopped the dining room floor or to fall over in admiration of my new hairstyle when he's got a major project going on at work? And I'm sure it's quite easy for him to forget to tell me what a fabulous mother I am and that he loves me more than life itself when he's busy trying to figure out how we're going to make the car payment before the end of the month.

A marriage really runs into trouble, however, when neither spouse's particular needs for love and attention are being met. As a consequence, both spouses feel cheated. Neither is inclined to put forth the effort to please the other, and the sorry stage is set for a downward-spiraling cycle of bitterness and resentment.

The solution here is to make that effort to meet your spouse's wants and needs first, even if it feels forced and even if it feels unfair. After all, it is in meeting your husband's needs that you will inspire him to meet yours. But your husband's particular needs for love and attention might be quite different from my husband's. To find out what he really wants, you will need to ask him. But this should be an easy project. What person wouldn't love to be asked, "What kinds of things can I do to make you feel loved?" The bonus for you is that once he has shared his needs with you, he'll be more inclined to ask what kinds of things he can do that will make you happy.

It's worth mentioning, too, that during a discussion of wants and needs with your spouse is no time to be shy or vague. If you think you might be more responsive to your husband's romantic overtures if he complimented your appearance or appreciated your work more frequently, do the guy a favor and tell him so! In my marriage, we've both reaped great benefits from sharing our specific wants, needs, and expectations with each other on a regular basis.

It has been my experience that sometimes, after talking and sharing our needs, especially if we've been feeling distant, things can feel a bit forced or even silly as we go about trying to please one another. Having a sense of humor loosens us both up a bit, though. Once, I told Dan that I really would like him to pay attention to little things and to compliment me more often. For a long while after that discussion, whenever he made a positive comment, after I smiled and thanked him, he would say

"Ka-ching!"—like he was putting money in the bank. Very cute. And accurate.

All kidding aside, though, our regular efforts at better communication and paying attention to one another's needs have been rewarded with a genuine closeness and loving intimacy between the two of us. That's what I call romance!

Date Night

B etween children, work schedules, and household obligations of all kinds, it can be very difficult for couples to find quiet time alone together on a regular basis. The trick, I have discovered, is to recognize spending time together as a priority, then to schedule it on a regular basis.

One of the most successful things I ever did early in our marriage was to establish a weekly "date night" with my husband. The secret to its success has been to keep it low-key, casual—and mandatory. We seldom use babysitters, but for the most part I've found that we don't need them. We have to be careful about the money we spend, but I've found that sharing special time together doesn't have to be expensive, either.

Here's how it works for us: We pick a night of the week and block it off. On that night, after the kids go to bed, we have dinner together. We keep the food simple (we even opt for takeout on occasion) and we usually watch a television show or a movie. That's it. It's not fancy. It's not too demanding. But it *is* mandatory. Though I frequently work in the evenings, I never work on our designated date night. Dan, too, respects this time by scheduling other activities around it.

Through the years, we've kept our date nights with newborns by our side, in the throes of family illness, and even once as I was beginning labor before delivering baby Gabrielle. There have also been times when we've been holding grudges or arguing all day and yet, since it's "date night," we still keep our "date." The forced time alone together breaks the ice, obliges us to talk with each other, maybe laugh a little, and finally, reconnect.

Evening dates might not work for everyone. I know of some couples that schedule breakfast together once a week or take walks together on certain afternoons. Whatever the details of your time together, though, I think it's important to make it a regular occurrence and to make it a priority. Your dates might not always be filled with passion and wild romance, and that's not really the point. You will both benefit from the opportunity to reconnect with one another away from outside pressures and obligations. And what's more, your commitment speaks volumes to the value you place on your relationship.

Dear Lord, thank you for the husband you have given to me. In the gift of our marriage, I see the genius of your divine plan for men, women, and the family. Because we are so different, we can work together so beautifully and in such complementary ways. But when

our differences become a source of conflict, fill our hearts again with the graces we received on our wedding day. Turn our thoughts toward you. Help us to love one another as you love us. Help us to forgive as you forgive. Help us to meet one another's needs with cheerful generosity. And remind us that it is through each other that you call each of us to greater holiness. Amen.

three

What Kind of Role Does a Catholic Mom Play in This Great Big World?

Not Everyone Is Catholic

I will never forget the night when my husband was working late and his brother stopped by for dinner. Before the meal, as we always do, we said grace. After the prayer, my then four-year-old Ambrose pointed accusingly at his uncle.

"You didn't say grace!" he shouted indignantly.

My brother-in-law, who professes no particular religious beliefs, simply answered, "That's right. I didn't."

But his inquisitor wanted more than a mere confession. "*Why* didn't you say grace?" Ambrose demanded to know.

All the children's eyes trained on their bewildered uncle. Now these are kids who before this time would generally walk around assuming that everyone they met was Catholic. They would hear about the post office being closed on Sunday and say, "Of course, it's closed. Because the mailman needs to go to Mass."

I could tell that my brother-in-law wasn't sure how I wanted him to handle the question, so I tried to spare him.

"Your uncle doesn't know our grace," I jumped in.

It was true, after all. Perhaps that wasn't exactly the primary reason their uncle hadn't joined us in saying grace, but it was surely not a lie and I hoped it might save us a bit of awkwardness. My ploy worked. For a moment, anyway. The kids nodded their heads in understanding and began to talk about something else.

After only a few mouthfuls of meatloaf, however, it became clear that Ambrose wasn't satisfied. He set down his fork and stared his uncle straight in the eye. Very slowly and skeptically, he asked him, "What grace *do* you say?"

My poor brother-in-law was trapped. What could he say? The uncle cried uncle. "I don't say any grace," he admitted.

A collective gasp of shock and disbelief ran around the table. *He doesn't say grace? He doesn't thank God for his food? What kind of guest had we invited to our table?*

That night my children's eyes were opened to the fact that not all the world believes and practices as we do.

I don't recall exactly how I explained the situation to the kids that particular evening, but that night my children's eyes were opened to the fact that not all the world believes and practices as we do. And, on the whole, that has not been a bad thing. It's opened up many opportunities for important discussions about our faith. It's also strengthened my children's resolve to pray for loved ones and others who don't share our faith, as well as for those who do.

I happen to be fortunate in that the non-Catholic members of our families aren't hostile to our beliefs. My e-mail tells me, however, that many young families find themselves battling the intrusions of hostile relatives as they attempt to raise their children in the Catholic faith. I can only imagine the trials that situation would present. I think it's important for children to maintain and develop relationships with extended family members, but it's even more important that their family's faith be respected.

If you suffer from antagonistic family members, I think you can and should set some ground rules for your relatives to follow. You are grown-ups, after all. You are the parents and you are in control of what and who you will allow to influence your children at an early age. Let family members know that comments that attack or disrespect the faith and values you are imparting to your children will not be tolerated in your home. While you can't make the rules about what kinds of things might be done or said in other people's homes, you can make the decision to avoid visiting there.

There's no need to be ugly about it, though. In fact, it would be a good idea to make every effort to be charitable and kind in your requests and your explanations. Be clear about the fact that you are not "punishing" anyone or denying them the right to see their nieces, nephews, or grandkids. You are only asking for decency and respect. You are only defending your own right to raise your children as you see fit. Should your family members choose to dishonor your reasonable requests, that would be their own unfortunate decision.

Either way, you should take full advantage of the opportunity for charity and growth this challenge presents to your family. Perhaps God has given you particu-

larly difficult family members because he knows how effi-
cacious your prayers on their behalf will be. Involve your
children in this act of charity by encouraging them to
join you in praying for those who don't share the gift of
their faith.

Knowing and loving people who don't share our faith
can also move us toward a greater appreciation of our
own gifts. Our faith truly is a gift from God. It's not something we can take personal credit for. That fact alone
should humble us and inspire us to intensify our prayers
on behalf of those who have not been so abundantly
blessed. Besides, you never know which of those non-
believing friends or family members is studying your good
example...and learning more than your words could ever
teach them.

Mother of Many

We live in a small town. Being one of the only larger families for miles around, the Bean family seems to have acquired somewhat of a celebrity status around these parts. In fact, when I meet another mom at the playground and attempt to introduce myself, more often than not she responds by telling me she already knows who I am. Then I'm left to wonder exactly *how* she knows. Were we out in public at some point when a friend elbowed this woman and whispered, "That's the crazy Bean family. They have eight kids *and* they homeschool!" followed by gasps all around? I guess I don't want to know.

Like most mothers of many, I sometimes do feel a little bit like a freak show. People gasp and whisper. They point fingers and count heads. We get it at the grocery store, the doctor's office, even sometimes at church. One afternoon not too long ago, I attended one of my oldest son Eamon's baseball games. I guess he hit a triple, but I missed it.

You see, once some of the other mothers figured out who I was, they surrounded me. Some of them stood staring, wide-eyed and slack-jawed. Others peppered me with questions like, "How much milk do you guys drink in a week? What do you drive—a school bus?" and, "Is your husband rich?" Some of them even skipped the niceties and got right to the point: "Are you crazy???"

It was embarrassing. I just wanted to watch my son play baseball like every other mother there. Sometimes I just want to be normal. I want to fit in.

Sometimes I just want to be normal. I want to fit in.

I don't usually go around seeking public attention, so when people react to my life with shock and disbelief, I often feel uncomfortable and embarrassed. I try not to take it too personally, though. We *are* different. We *do* stand out. Many times other people just aren't going to understand us and they *are* going to be shocked.

When I'm tempted to feel resentful or offended by others' consternation, however, I sometimes find it helpful to recall a time when I was stunned by someone else's life. Have you ever felt absolutely astounded by someone else's life circumstances or accomplishments? How on earth do people ever manage to climb Mount Everest, for instance? Or cut off their own arms when they're pinned beneath a rock in an abandoned cave? And how on earth did those pioneer women ever manage to have a gang of children, grow their own food, and make their own clothes with no running water or electricity?

If you think about it, your initial reaction of shock in these situations isn't really a put-down. Even though your stunned expression might make these people feel uncomfortable if you met them, your shock and awe are really just a form of admiration. When we encounter something so vastly different from our own experiences, we're curious. We want to know how they do it. And why they do it. And isn't it just terribly awful? And if not, then what exactly is it like?

As much as I understand people's shocked reactions, I do commiserate with mothers of large families who just want to fit in sometimes. But let's consider what that would mean for mothers of many children. To meet the modern world's standards of "normal," we'd have to give up some of our kids. And we'd surely need to make certain that our faith isn't a tangible, noticeable part of who we are or how we live in any kind of way. Think how bland and empty and lonely that kind of life seems in comparison to the way we're living now.

As much as we might complain about it, most of us women who stand out for our family choices don't really want to be normal. Not if it means lowering our standards for ourselves and our families. Besides, "fitting in" isn't God's plan for most of us, anyway:

> "You are the light of the world. A city built on a hill cannot be hid. No one after lighting a lamp puts it under the bushel basket, but on the lampstand, and it gives light to all in the house. In the same way, let your light shine before others, so that they may see your good works and give glory to your Father in heaven." (Mt 5:14–16)

Rats, right? As it turns out, God isn't calling us to a life of social comfort and ease. He is calling us to stick out a bit, and to be uncomfortable for his sake. Knowing that God wills it might not make it any easier to be the odd man out. But the good news is that there are abundant rewards for those of us who do persevere in the face of adversity.

Too Much...and Not Enough

I think that most at-home mothers, especially those with higher educations or professional backgrounds, struggle at some point or other with the feeling that they are letting their minds and their skills wither away, particularly in the early years. Many of us start out with high ideals. I for one yearned desperately to be able to stay home with our first child the first year after she was born, but was unable to.

When at last I was able to quit my job and embrace the full-time mothering I had longed for, I suffered through some terribly lonely, misunderstood, verrrrry looooong days. In fact, at the ends of some days, I felt downright disillusioned. I suppose I had known beforehand that staying home was all about babies and babbling, messes and mayhem, all day every day. But until I actually did it, I don't think I fully appreciated the fact that staying home truly was *all about babies and babbling, messes and mayhem, all day every day.* It felt like too much. And not enough. All at the same time.

Here's the thing, though. At the time I was struggling with my longing for something more, I was scarcely adjusted to the something I had. When I got married, I was quite happy to change my *it's all about me* attitude to *it's all about us*. That was a fun kind of adventure that I could call a sacrifice. It felt grown-up and special. And it was a pretty easy transition, because focusing on myself and my husband just so happened to be an extension of the *it's all about me* attitude that had served me so well for so many years.

With motherhood, though, and with staying home in particular, I quickly learned that it wasn't about me, after all. In fact, it wasn't even a little bit about me. It was *all about the babies*. And I was supposed to love that. Sometimes, all the blah-blah-blah I had read about the beauty of a mother's self-giving love and about the magnificent joys of sacrificing for the sake of others would pop into my mind during a trying moment, and I would try to think all the wonderful thoughts that had so enraptured me before. But during those moments, all those high ideals made me want to do was spit fire.

During those moments, all those high ideals made me want to do was spit fire.

During the early years, it helps to keep in mind that you're in the throes of making a profound and life-changing adjustment. Be patient with yourself and give yourself the time you need to do it completely and do it well. Also, be aware that any attempts to assess your situation before you've fully adjusted will be tainted by the overwhelming newness of your motherhood.

Now that I've said that, I must say that I fully and completely recognize a mother's need for "something else." We all have gifts—yes, mothers do too—and we are called to use them and to share them. But can a mother use and share her gifts beyond her family without shirking her primary responsibilities? Of course she can.

For example, by keeping up with and pursuing my love of writing, I've managed through the years to find a worthwhile outlet for my own need for creativity without sacrificing my primary vocation of marriage and motherhood. In fact, I find that my writing about faith and motherhood forces me to reflect and to step back and see the "big picture" on a regular basis. Doing so helps to keep me focused on those things that are most important to me. I appreciate more of the little things and precious moments that make up my days as a busy mother simply because I'm often observing and scrutinizing these experiences from the perspective of a writer.

What's more, there are times when working on a writing project in my head while doing other work in the house occupies my mind during what would otherwise be painfully dull moments. When I'm struggling to find the right words to conclude an essay I'm working on, I play with words and ideas in my head while I clean the bathroom or do the laundry. In the end, if I'm lucky, I have not just a sparkling shower or a pile of clean, folded clothes, but the perfect wording as well.

Not everyone is called to be a writer, of course, but there's much to be gained from many different kinds of outside pursuits. With just a bit of thought and creativity, many kinds of talents can be explored without sacrificing family responsibilities. A teacher can tutor students part time. A cook can experiment with recipes. A quilter can stay up past her children's bedtimes creating masterpieces that will become family heirlooms.

I would surely encourage young mothers who feel the need to pursue their gifts and spend some time in roles outside of motherhood. Just bear in mind that, whatever your other gifts or callings may be, you are the only mother your children will ever have. And you are your husband's only wife. That alone is hugely important. Know that being a wife and mother are the most important things you will ever do. And, regardless of outside pursuits and distractions, being "just" a wife and a mother always *is* enough. The "something more" we mothers sometimes seek will never be the "everything" we alone are called to be to our families.

Charity Begins at Home

It can be hard to keep our priorities straight when there are so many good causes and charitable opportunities out there vying for our time and attention. But consider this: If God has made you a wife and a mother, that's your vocation. As a wife and mother, your energies and attentions belong first and foremost to your own family. That's right. They get dibs and they should come first. Always.

Of course, that doesn't mean that we can never involve ourselves with worthy projects outside of our homes and our families, but it does mean that outside responsibilities should be considered in relation to how much they will affect our primary responsibilities.

It's taken me some time to come to this conclusion. Personally, I like to be busy. When I was in high school, I thrived on being overly involved in any number of clubs, organizations, and extracurricular activities, some of which I hardly even enjoyed or cared about. My activities didn't slow down much when I got to college, either. I did try to focus my non-academic energies on pro-life work in particular, though.

Then came my marriage and my children. And some more children. And then a few more. I tried to maintain my packed agenda but found that whiny toddlers at organizational meetings and exploding diapers in the middle of pro-life counselor training sessions really slowed me down. Besides, it seemed like everyone we knew was busy having babies and, more often than not, it was these immediate friends and neighbors who required my "extra" attention. There were new moms in need of homemade dinners brought to their houses, and there were lonely, frustrated moms in need of friendly visits or extended phone calls.

There was always some worthy needy person outside of my home who seemed to have a "right" to my attention. Now, I don't know about you, but I find cleaning someone else's bathroom a much more attractive prospect than cleaning my own. There's just so much more satisfaction and a real feeling of accomplishment in stepping in and helping someone else in need. What's more, my husband almost never remembers to thank me for spending my entire day taking care of his children. But when I offer to babysit for a friend in need, the appreciation can be overwhelming.

The important thing to keep in mind, though, is that however worthwhile the work you do for others may be, no one can replace you at home. Your children have only one mother—that's you. Your husband has only one wife—that's you.

It can be a tricky balance, though. Once, when a friend of mine went through a personal crisis, I followed my instincts, dropped everything in my own life, and made myself completely available to her. For weeks. She surely needed my help and friendship, but my generosity to my friend began to take its toll on my own family. While I cooked for my friend's family, my kids were surviving on peanut-butter-and-jelly sandwiches and potato chips. While I visited my friend and spent long hours on the phone with her, the children frequently suffered from a lack of motherly attention and became unruly. My own housework didn't get done. And my ever-patient

However worthwhile the work you do for others may be, no one can replace you at home.

husband felt he had little claim to my energy, attention, and affection at the end of the day, when I was exhausted from all the "help" I was giving to others.

Ultimately, I had to admit that however crucial my friend's need seemed to be, what I was doing was imbalanced. It was wrong of me to give to others at the expense of my own family for such an extended period of time. God doesn't want that kind of charity.

This doesn't mean that anyone who is a mother should never give of her time and energy to others. We are all members of communities and we do have a Christian obligation to respond generously to the needs of others. I am merely cautioning over-achieving mothers to seek balance between their at-home obligations and outside activities.

I once knew a formerly over-achieving mother who learned this lesson the hard way. After years of volunteering at her kids' school and saying "yes" to every demand any person asked of her time for worthy causes, she finally suffered burnout. She made a daring decision: She decided to make a habit of giving people a polite but firm "no" every time they requested any kind of commitment from her. She explained that she could always think about it some more and change her mind later if she did decide that it would be a good use of her time. But the immediate and automatic "no" freed her from the sense of obligation that used to compel her to say "yes" to as many things as humanly possible.

I like her strategy but have never felt confident or comfortable enough to employ it myself. Since most of my outside activity temptations are on a personal level, I find it simplest to focus on maintaining balance between my family's basic needs for my energy and attention and the needs I see in others. I make sure I treat my own family's needs as a priority.

For example, you might decide that having dinner together as a family is an important part of your daily routine. Or maybe your husband really counts on the two of you being able to spend Sundays or most evenings together. You can make these family needs a priority and participate only in those activities that don't interfere with them.

I will warn you, though. As your family grows, you'll get busier and will likely find yourself less and less able to participate in outside activities that don't include them. This is perfectly all right and not something anyone should ever feel guilty about. When I'm tempted to feel guilty or to take on a new worthy project, I remind myself that my family's needs should always be my first priority. Especially while there are small children in my home. It's my job. One that God himself has given to me. Charity really does begin at home.

Dear Lord, thank you for the gift of my Catholic faith. I never want to take for granted the graces I receive in the sacraments or the great source of comfort, encouragement, and inspiration that I have in you. Make me a worthy disciple. Enable me to lead others to you through my own faithful example. Help me to use my gifts to save souls, encourage virtue, and bring your good news to others. Give me strength that I might never be ashamed to share your love with others and to bear witness to my faith. Give me the grace to serve you by serving my family and others and help me to live a faithful life, that I might one day find my reward with you in heaven. Amen.

four

How Can I Get on Top of the Housework When It Feels Like I'm Smothering Under It?

Housework Burnout

Oh, the never-ending housework! It simply must be done, right? There's laundry, meals, general cleanup, not to mention the floors, the windows, the dishes, the inside of the refrigerator, and that grungy spot on the floor behind the toilet.

I think the single most frustrating thing about housework is the fact that it's *never* done. When it comes to keeping house, there's just no resting on your dust-mop laurels. You know how it goes. Just as you close the lid on an empty clothes hamper, some child in your home is going to fall in a mud puddle or vomit in his sheets.

And one of the most exasperating things about housework is that if you do it right...no one notices. After years of marriage, I think I've finally come to terms with the fact that, as much as I would love it, my husband is never going to come home from work at the end of the day and gasp, "Wow, honey, that floor looks fantastic!" even if I did spend all afternoon mopping it. It's only when the grime on the bathroom counter starts to build up or some small person has trouble finding a clean pair of socks that you're likely to hear a word about your housekeeping skills.

Housework is about maintenance. It's about keeping up, plugging away, and damage control. What I think too many people fail to realize is that for a stay-at-home mother, just having her house look exactly the same at the end of the day as it did at the beginning is a *major accomplishment*.

For a stay-at-home mother, just having her house look the same at the end of the day as it did at the beginning is a major accomplishment.

I have no magic solutions. Adam and Eve did eat that apple, you know, and this surely isn't the Garden of Eden. We feeble humans must earn our bread by the sweat of our brows. But I do have a few pointers to share on the subject of housework that frustrated homemakers might find helpful:

MAINTENANCE IS KEY. Cleaning house is an investment of your precious time and energy. You should treat it that way and maintain your hard work as much as possible. And you have every right to insist that your family members do the same. If you spent all morning cleaning out and organizing a family closet, do not allow anyone, including yourself, to toss any old thing in there afterwards. Spending a few minutes each day sorting through and clearing out those spots in your home that tend toward disorder will save you hours of work in the long run. Regularly wiping down the shelves inside your refrigerator will postpone the need for a major scrub-down. A quick daily wiping down of bathroom surfaces will spare you a time-consuming scrubbing project as well.

KIDS SHOULD HELP. This much I know: Modern-day kids are spoiled. My own included. If you've studied history, you know what I'm talking about. Just consider how much work was expected of the average child a century ago. They hauled wood. They cooked meals. They cleaned floors. They cared for livestock. Many of us have children who do these things today, but I think most of us have to admit that our kids live more leisurely lives than children of past generations. We all do. When I read the *Little House* series by Laura Ingalls Wilder, I get tired just reading about what Ma Ingalls accomplished in an average day.

The point is, however, that we shouldn't feel guilty about requiring our children's help with household tasks. They are sure to complain along the way, but in the long run, we all benefit from the shared responsibility. Children learn the importance of hard work and cooperation, gain valuable life skills, and enjoy the boost of self-esteem that comes from being a valuable, contributing member of the household. And we, of course, get the help we need.

If years of trial and error have taught me nothing else, however, they have surely taught me that giving children responsibility for household tasks does not take Mom off the hook entirely. Unfortunately, it's not quite as simple as handing them the brooms, sprays, and brushes and then sitting down with our feet up. We have to teach them how to do the work we require and *then* we have to follow through with inspection to make sure they do the jobs to the best of their ability.

This does take commitment. I sometimes find it tempting to do all the housework myself so that it will be done the way I like and I won't have to listen to anyone's whiny complaints. I try to remember, though, that I'm in a long-term battle here with long-term goals. With children for helpers, I do have to relax my standards a bit. And I surely do have to combat the grumpies now and then. But, ultimately, I do believe that if I take the time and make the effort to teach my children to be helpful— truly helpful—around the house, the shared load will make me a happier homemaker in the end.

PICK YOUR BATTLES. Though people sometimes e-mail me looking for one, there really is no one master list of the housekeeping chores that must be done on a regular basis for all households. Of course, a certain amount of cleanliness and order are required for any happy home, but in the end, each of us has only twenty-four hours in a day and most of us do *not* spend all of our waking hours organizing and cleaning. We have to prioritize. Each of us must decide which tasks are important enough to ourselves and to our families to warrant spending time doing them on a regular basis. The final list of must-be-done chores will be different for every family.

Don't decide that the curtains must be washed every other week and the garbage cans scrubbed on Saturdays simply because that's what your mother always did. Those things might have been important to her and to her household, but are they to you? Make your personalized housework list carefully, thoughtfully, and with input from all members of the family. Ask yourself what you can and cannot live with. Ask your husband what matters most to him. And ask the kids what's important to them as well. You might be surprised.

Ask yourself what you can and cannot live with.

I'll share an example. I've always been a notoriously terrible ironer. Early on in my marriage, I purchased an iron and an ironing board because that's what good wives do. But then I let the ironing just pile up and sit there…because that's what I did. I developed a guilt complex until one afternoon when I got our two small children to nap at the same time and I decided to tackle the problem. This was the day, I told myself, that I would finally be that "good wife" I was sure my husband was missing. I spent the afternoon spritzing, steaming, pressing, and creasing.

When my husband arrived home from work that day, I was so excited to show him my accomplishment. But his reaction wasn't exactly what I expected. "That's nice," he shrugged. "But why did you waste your time doing the *ironing?*"

What? Could it be that he didn't care about the ironing after all? As it turned out, that was exactly the case. And he didn't need to say another word. We invested in some wrinkle-resistant pants and shirts for him to wear to work, I became diligent about removing clothing from the dryer promptly and giving it that all-important shake before hanging, and then I—oh, the joy!—retired my ironing board to the outdoor storage shed. It is now reserved for special occasions, and I spend that saved time doing tasks that my family actually cares about.

Clearing Clutter

We live in a small house, so through the years I have learned to "do without" and "throw it out." In my experience, nothing makes a mother crabbier than that claustrophobic feeling that comes from being surrounded by piles of stuff. Junk. Things that are so buried beneath other things that you have long ago forgotten they even exist, so there is *no chance in the world* that you are ever going to actually use them.

The key to controlling clutter, I have discovered through many frustrating, clutter-battling years, is never to let it get the upper hand in the first place. Find out where clutter tends to accumulate in your home and check these spots regularly. Do school papers and unopened mail pile up on the kitchen counters? Spending two minutes each day sorting, saving, and throwing away will save you an hour or so of digging out at the end of a month's time. Do your keys and other random items continually wind up on top of a particular coffee table? Find hooks or containers for storing these things and go through the rest of the pile on a daily basis.

I once read a book that advised homemakers to make their possessions *earn* a place in their homes. By actually being used. Most of us have too much stuff. Why add to the piles? I never hold onto anything for any other reason than it is actually useful and is actually used. If you are serious about ridding your home of clutter, this means you simply must throw out old newspapers and magazines, even if there is that one recipe or article you keep meaning to clip. Let's be honest here. If you're anything like me, you're never going to get around to clipping it. And even if you do, you'll lose it under some pile or other and never get around to making it. If I am really interested in a recipe I've found, I make the effort to clip and store it right away. Anything else I just throw away and never even think about again.

But kids love to collect stuff too, don't they? What do you do when the clutter monsters in your household are your own children? You set a good example and you ask them politely to go through their things and throw away whatever isn't worth keeping. If that doesn't work (and I'll be honest with you here—I know of very few people for whom that strategy *would* actually work), you must take matters into your own hands. This home is your space, Mom. Claim it. Take control of it.

This home is your space, Mom. Take control of it.

Even those of us who try to keep childhood materialism at bay have to admit on occasion that *our* kids, too, have too much stuff. I try to keep the kids on top of their bedroom spaces with daily cleanups and a weekly deeper cleaning. Sometimes, however, as the kids are reluctant to part with their "precious stuff" that they never use or enjoy, the piles just build up anyway. That's how I know it's time for a "Black Bag Day."

On Black Bag Day, I wait until the baby's down for a nap and then put on a long movie for the older kids. Then, while they sit mesmerized by the flickering screen, I tiptoe upstairs to their bedrooms with a large box of black garbage bags. Then, I have no mercy.

If no one plays with it or hasn't in a while, it goes in the bag. If it's ugly, if it's broken, if it's plastic, if it's missing pieces, if it smells bad, if I am not sure what it is or think perhaps it might be alive...out it goes. Even if Great Auntie So-and-So just sent this brand new "perfect" doodad for the kids last week, even if it is the only one of its kind, even if it might be popular again some day, even if it was fun or useful or nice once upon a time...out it goes.

The kids don't even notice me lugging the giant bags out to the trash or to the van for giving away. And afterward, they surely don't miss the stuff that caused the cluttered mess in their room. Let's face it, our kids have no idea what specific things make up the bulk of what's in their overflowing toy boxes. After a Black Bag Day, there's plenty of clean, open space for playing with the toys that they actually use and care about.

Remember that the same tough rules apply to grown-up stuff too. Be ruthless. Be callous. Be as unsentimental as humanly possible. If you don't use it—and let's be honest here—get rid of it. Give it away or throw it away. Things you don't use or enjoy have no right to claim precious space within your home. I am here to tell you that I have been just plain cold-hearted about saving things for years now and never once have I found myself wanting or missing an item I tossed in a fit of de-cluttering. After all, it's just stuff. And life just feels so good when you clear away the piles of clutter.

Virus Crisis

Even in the happiest of homes, disaster sometimes strikes. It usually comes in the form of some kind of illness or other. Sometimes an evil stomach virus runs through the household and, while caring for her family of patients, a mother finds herself sleepless for days on end. At other times, pregnancy woes might claim a mother's own good health, and she's the one who collapses on the couch.

The best advice I can offer families in "virus crisis" and moms in sleep deprivation is to treat sleep-deprived days like the "emergency" situations they are. Even if you're not the one who's sick, if you've been up all night with a feverish baby or a vomiting child, your energy and ability are sure to be compromised from lack of proper rest. I would contend that situations like these are precisely why God gave us the wonderful gifts of baby swings, DVD players, and frozen foods.

You shouldn't feel guilty about using emergency measures to survive an emergency situation. Let the kids watch TV, or enlist an older one to read aloud to the younger ones while you and the baby rest for a bit during the day. Also, I'd recommend that you don't do any unnecessary chores. For example, *must* you do laundry—or could the

family get through another day with what they are wearing or what's in their dressers? *Must* you go to the supermarket—or could you manage dinner (even a funny
dinner) with whatever you have in the pantry?

I would further encourage you to appeal to your
children's "inner hero." One recent winter I suffered a
terrible bout of influenza. Though I struggled with the
idea of letting go of my "Super Mom" status, I was
amazed by how willingly my children rose to the occasion with extra help when I let them know that I needed them and how much I
appreciated their contributions.
My husband helped out as his
work schedule allowed, but he
would also sometimes give the
kids a "pep talk" before he left
for work about how it was going
to be a hard day for Mama and
how much she really needed
each of them to pitch in. This
worked wonders. The fact is,
most kids really do want to be
helpful and they are extra motivated if you present it to
them as a grown-up responsibility.

*Most kids really do
want to be helpful
and they are extra
motivated if you
present it to them
as a grown-up
responsibility.*

I know it can be hard to believe while you are in the
midst of it, but whether you are suffering from pregnan-
cy-related sickness or a common virus, your time of trial
really is a passing phase in your family life, and one from
which you will all benefit in the long run. Sometimes the

hardest thing is to just accept that God wills us to do nothing right now. Especially for those of us who are perfectionists, doers, and controllers, the biggest sacrifice can be in just letting things go. Just lying on the couch. Just turning on the TV. Just opening cans for dinner or letting someone else handle the meals.

It wounds our pride to admit we're helpless, and we can grow weary of relying on others' charity, but sometimes we simply can't do otherwise. What's more, when mothers are sick, their husbands, children, and friends have a great opportunity to practice patience and charity.

It might also be helpful to bear in mind that the sick have tremendous power in their suffering. Think of the many saints who spent their final years in prolonged illness. Why would God allow it? Because he knows what value there can be for all souls in suffering.

I think that some mothers feel guilty about asking their families to pitch in during trying times. I would argue, though, that teaching children to recognize and come to the aid of those in need is a valuable life lesson and your home is the perfect place to teach it. You can discuss with them how Jesus calls us to serve one another and point out that when they take on extra responsibilities during times of illness, they are "visiting the sick" and performing other "works of mercy."

Thinking in terms of the works of mercy can add a bit of levity to your virus crisis as well. One recent spring, my entire family fell prey to a vicious stomach virus during the week that my second son was to receive his First

Communion. At the time, I recast the works of mercy as follows:

The Corporal Works of Mercy: Stomach Flu Version

1. Visit the sick.

This is an easy one. Rocking a crabby, tummy-achy baby counts. And so does sitting late-night vigil with older kids and sharing vomit horror stories from your own childhood. And watching *Thomas the Tank Engine* and reading *Gossie and Gertie* over and over and over and over again, until you think your brains might just liquefy and come oozing out from your ears, had better count, too.

2. Feed the hungry.

Sometimes this is a seriously bad idea. For example, you might practice feeding the hungry by taking the entire family out to eat at a Chinese restaurant to celebrate one son's First Communion day. Then, in the early morning hours of the following day, you might just find yourself hunched over the bathtub rinsing partially digested chicken teriyaki, fried rice, and pork spareribs out of someone's bed sheets. Do not ask how I know this. Just learn from me, people.

3. Give drink to the thirsty.

Aside from occasional sips of ginger ale, this one is also often a bad idea. Especially strawberry milk. Pink is a very pretty color, but not under these particular circumstances.

4. *Clothe the naked.*

I struggle to keep up with this one. There are the towels, bed linens, and middle-of-the-night pajama changes. And then there's what happened to Gabrielle immediately following the First Communion Mass. Without going into too much detail, I will just tell you that the situation required a complete removal of dress, shoes, tights, and diaper, followed by a total body "scrub-down" with baby wipes. Then the dress, tights, and diaper needed to be wrapped tightly in a plastic bag and deposited waaaaaay in the back of the van. Then, of course, came the clothing of the naked, for which I was hopelessly unprepared. My needy naked daughter rode home from Mass wearing a diaper, her coat, and a hair bow.

5. *Bury the dead.*

It hasn't gotten quite that serious around here yet. The only "burial" we had was when I asked Dan to stop the van on the way home from Mass so that I could dump the above-mentioned plastic bag into an outdoor trash receptacle. I think I paid about $5.00 for that dress at a consignment store three years ago. Yup. Totally worth it.

In the midst of family crises, as unbelievable as it might seem, it can also be helpful to remember that life will return to normal someday. In the meantime, try to lower your expectations and standards just a bit and remain open to reaping the benefits that might be found in doing exactly that.

During my own horrific bout with influenza, I noted the sacrifices my family and I were being forced to make in the face of my illness and reflected on them as follows:

The kids are eating a lot of frozen, processed, and canned foods.

Thank you, God, for the abundance of good food we have. Thank you for the work that provides for us so very well, in sickness and in health.

I can't stand up for very long without feeling weak and tired.

Thank you, God, for the opportunity to recognize the importance of focusing on one small task at a time. Thank you for the chance to discover the peace there can be in simply feeding the baby his yogurt—one small spoonful at a time—without even *thinking* of doing anything else.

I can't keep up with the housework.

Thank you, God, for showing me that the earth does not in fact cease spinning on its axis if the stairs aren't swept for two days. Or four.

I am frustrated and exhausted.

Thank you, God, for the reminder of what a precious gift our good health is and how very much we take it for granted all the other days of the year. Thank you for the gentle nudge toward greater charity for those who suffer more serious and chronic illnesses.

The kids have been doing way too little schoolwork and watching way too much TV.

Thank you, God, for the reminder that we all fall short of our own standards and expectations sometimes. That we are all works in progress. And that sometimes a mom needs to accept a little help.

This morning, while Eamon was making breakfast, Stephen accidentally called him "Mama" and something inside me wanted to cry.

Thank you, God, for the precious gift of a helpful husband and older children who are eager to take on new jobs and pitch in during my moment of crisis. Thank you for capable, cheerful children, and for the reminder to recognize their accomplishments.

I am in pain.

Thank you, God, for the opportunity to unite my small sufferings with yours. Thank you for the chance to suffer here on earth where our tiny aches and pains have greater value than I could ever know.

The Inevitable End-of-the-Day Chaos

O h, no! Is it dinnertime already? I've tried hard to fight this truth, but this far into my homemaking career, I think that I finally must admit: When it comes to cooking for a family, planning ahead really does make your life easier.

In organizational books and magazine articles, I've always read that it's helpful to plan at least a week's worth of meals at a time. But since this practice takes work and discipline, I tried getting by with just winging it at the grocery store and muddling my way through a week's worth of dinnertimes. Alas! My genius plan didn't always work out as well as I intended. I spent too much money on non-nutritious convenience foods. There were too many emergency trips to the grocery store for recipes I decided to make at the last minute. And there were way too many late-afternoon panic attacks as I fretted, "What on earth am I going to make for dinner?"

Ultimately, planning meals ahead of time, however painful you find its lack of spontaneity, saves you time, money, energy, and anxiety. I actually enjoy cooking and, like many moms, have always collected recipes. With my old way of approaching dinnertime, however, I never seemed to get around to trying any of those recipes on a regular basis.

Let's face it. When it's 5:00 P.M., you have no real plan for dinner, and your pantry is filled with only random staple ingredients, you just are not going to attempt Chicken Parmagiana with homemade tomato sauce and olives. You're going to have frozen pizza, pancakes, or cheese omelets for dinner. Your family will be fed and you will have avoided that extra bit of preplanning, but you know how much more enjoyable and more balanced your family's meal could have been with just a little bit of forethought.

Every mother needs to come up with a personalized system that works for her, but here's how I usually handle meal planning and preparation:

At the beginning of the week, I spend some time browsing through favorite cookbooks and online recipe sites. Using a combination of old favorites and at least one new recipe to try, I make up a grocery list of the ingredients I'll need. Taking the family calendar into consideration, I plan which meals and desserts I will make on which days. As I tend to double recipes and cook in large portions, I usually plan at least one dinner of leftovers per week. It's helpful to plan the leftover dinner or a quick and simple meal on days that I anticipate will be extra busy. Preplanning also enables me to anticipate using leftover rice or cooked chicken for another meal, and incorporating "planned leftovers" saves me cooking time the second time around. I fill in my list with the rest of the staples I'll need to get me through the week, including breakfast and lunch foods.

After the shopping comes fitting cooking dinner into my day. If I know what we're having for dinner when I get up in the morning, I can chop vegetables or prepare side dishes during a morning break or the baby's afternoon nap. That way, when the inevitable end-of-the-day chaos descends upon me, throwing dinner together becomes just a bit simpler and quicker.

I might add a final note about cooking with children. Kids love to cook and, if taught properly, they can be a real help in the kitchen. Some mothers I know assign a child the job of being "helper of the day" for each day of the week. That helper is then the only one who's allowed in the kitchen with mom during dinner preparations.

Kids love to cook and, if taught properly, they can be a real help in the kitchen.

Personally, I enjoy cooking with my kids but find that dinnertime is often just too stressful for that kind of "help." You know, the kind of "help" that dips sucked-on fingers in the cheese sauce, drops eggs on the floor, and pours a container of salt into the pasta pot. To avoid bursting a blood vessel, I tend to relegate the younger children's cooking projects to other times of day (baking muffins in the morning or a dessert in the afternoon, for instance). The only "helpers" I enlist at dinnertime are older kids who can actually be trusted to stir a pot of gravy or peel the potatoes properly. Younger children can still be my dinnertime helpers by setting the table, pouring milk, and keeping the baby happy.

When it comes to having children help you in the kitchen, try to keep in mind the long-term rewards you'll reap for the time and patience you spend now. Many times I bit my tongue and stood back as my oldest daughter Kateri learned to measure, mix, peel, and pour years ago, as a preschooler. Today, at eleven years old, however, Kateri can bread the chicken and peel and chop the vegetables for dinner without any kind of adult supervision. She also frequently bakes up a batch of brownies or chocolate chip cookies entirely independently, from start to finish. That's what I call sweet success!

Dear Lord, thank you for always providing so abundantly for my family's material needs. Thank you for our family home, for our food and clothing, and for the many modern conveniences and possessions with which you have blessed us. Help me to use these blessings for the good of my family and to keep the "things" that must be sorted, organized, stored, cleaned, swept, dusted, and vacuumed from overwhelming me. Remind me of

your Blessed Mother Mary's humble service in attending to the Holy Family's material needs, and give me the grace to follow her good example. May my family's home here on earth be a happy, holy place that assists us on our way to live with you forever in heaven. Amen.

five

How Can I Make Our Faith an Integral Part of Family Life?

Our Year with God

Sure, you attend Mass once a week. You enroll your kids in your parish's religious education program. You might even teach them their catechism or supplement their schooling by preparing them yourself, at home, to receive the sacraments. Even when we do all these things, however, many of us are left wondering how to make our Catholic faith more of an everyday part of who we are, and how to make our faith's traditions more accessible to our children. Well, the good news is that living and learning about your Catholic faith at home need not be complicated. It can even be quite simple and a whole lot of fun.

Besides teaching them basic catechism lessons, one way we can instill faith in children is to follow the liturgical calendar and observe various feast days that are recognized within the Church. Beyond the well-known observances of Easter, Christmas, Lent, and Advent, there are a wide variety of lesser-known feasts and special days to learn about and celebrate together.

I would caution you not to try to celebrate everything, though. The Catholic Church is over two thousand years old and abounds with many feasts, customs, and traditions. If you try to do everything, you'll suffer liturgical burnout in the first few days. I'd encourage you to take a look at a liturgical calendar for yourself and then focus on particular feasts and observances that appeal to you. These observances don't need to be fancy or complicated. One easy way to approach living the liturgical year is to choose one seasonal event or activity a month to celebrate together at home. Simply adding those twelve Church-related events to your family calendar will greatly enrich your faith life and help to make Catholicism a living and real experience for all members of the family. To start you thinking, I'll share a few observances that my family has especially enjoyed over the years:

January

January 1: Solemnity of Mary, Mother of God

I used to think it odd to have a high feast day for Mary on the first of the year. Did the Church really think that after a late night of New Year's revelry people would be inclined to drag themselves out of bed and get to Mass? But last year I read a timely article in the *National Catholic Register* that changed my perspective. Secular New Year observances encourage us to find ways to improve ourselves; people make New Year's resolutions to lose weight, quit smoking, and cut up their credit cards. Shouldn't our spiritual New Year observances encourage personal improvement as well? And isn't a focus on Mary, the Mother of God and our mother in heaven, a wonderful way to do exactly that?

On New Year's Day, in addition to any secular resolutions we might make, I encourage the family (and myself!) to make spiritual resolutions as well. Anything goes, as long as it's a step toward improvement. You might add more opportunities for confession or adoration to your calendar in the New Year. You might challenge your children to add a decade of the Rosary to their daily prayers or to work on a particular bad habit, such as failing to obey promptly, talking back, or being impatient. Then the important part is to make a point of sharing your resolutions with Our Lady at Mass on January 1 and asking for her help in keeping them. Mary is a good mother, you can remind the children. If we ask for her help, she will not let us down.

After Mass, we share a special New Year's dinner with a nice tablecloth, candles, and real wine glasses as part of the place settings for everyone—right down to the toddlers. If giving real glasses to little ones makes you nervous, stock up on cheap ones from a yard sale or the dollar store. In my experience, however, the special feeling of everyone drinking and toasting the New Year and our spiritual resolutions with "grown-up" glasses far outweighs any worries about potentially broken glassware.

In our house, we vary the New Year's menu, but you simply must have proper toasting beverages for everyone. Champagne and sparkling cider are traditional fare, but if you are feeling more adventurous, try this easy, delicious, lovely-to-look-at, non-alcoholic punch:

New Year's Punch

3½ liters ginger ale

2 quarts orange juice

2 oranges, sliced into rounds

20 maraschino cherries

Pour ginger ale and orange juice into a large punch bowl and stir gently. Float sliced orange rounds on top of punch and arrange the cherries on top of the orange slices.

February

Lent

The Church teaches that Lent is a time of increased prayer, fasting, and almsgiving. When introducing children to Lent, I find it especially helpful to focus on observing these three different parts of the season. We sit down together and talk about our Lenten plans. Every child's input is listened to, but when it comes to whole-family Lenten commitments, Mom gets the final say-so.

Prayer

Spend a bit of time together examining your family's prayer life. Have bedtime or morning prayers become so routine that they aren't meaningful anymore? In what ways might you add something to your daily regimen? You might decide to focus on reading Scripture together on a daily basis. This can be as simple as getting a children's Bible and setting aside time to read one story from it each day. Perhaps you can add the Rosary, the Angelus, or another traditional prayer to your daily routine. In addition, you can decide on a particular intention you want to pray for during this time. In the past, my children have really responded to the idea of praying for our troops overseas. They cheerfully added to their daily prayers knowing our soldiers would be benefiting from their efforts.

Fasting

I think this is the part of Lent most of us tend to focus on. "What are you giving up for Lent this year?" we ask one another. While I encourage the children to make some personal sacrifice during Lent that they may or may not choose to share with me, we always make a family sacrifice as well. We usually wind up giving up sweets and some television or computer time, but you might want to expand your idea of fasting a bit. Maybe your family could fast from angry words or complaining for Lent. This is a little trickier to enforce than simply not buying cookies for six weeks, but it can be fruitful. The key is to talk about the goal frequently.

Almsgiving

Children are naturally charitable creatures, and I think they take to almsgiving most readily. Each year, we choose a charity to benefit from our Lenten sacrifices. Perhaps your parish sponsors a "rice bowl" project during Lent where children can save up donations for starving people in other countries. I tend to think that local charities feel more real to children, and we've chosen nearby mission organizations, soup kitchens, and crisis pregnancy centers for our donations in the past. Once we've chosen a beneficiary, the children help to decorate and label a coffee can and we place it in a prominent location. Then, in addition to encouraging the children's own personal donations, each time we come home from the grocery store, I place the money we *would have* spent on things like ice cream, cookies, or candy into the can. At Easter time, the children love to count up the cash and help to send off our donation.

March

March 19: Feast of St. Joseph

I confess. I love St. Joseph's day. It's such a welcome respite from the rigors of Lent that the children and I look forward to it every year.

Besides reading and discussing parts of St. Joseph's life from the Bible, we usually make a special treat. Traditional Italian pastries such as St. Joseph's Cream Puffs are just the thing!

St. Joseph's Cream Puffs

Puffs:

 1 cup water

 ⅓ cup butter

 1 tablespoon sugar

 grated rind of 1 lemon

 pinch of salt

 1 cup sifted flour

 4 large eggs at room temperature

 1 tablespoon vanilla

Filling:

 2 cups ricotta cheese

 ½ cup confectioner's sugar

 ½ teaspoon vanilla

 ¼ teaspoon ground cinnamon

 ⅓ cup mini chocolate chips

 2 tablespoons finely chopped pistachios

 confectioners' sugar for sprinkling on top

For the cream puffs: Mix the water, butter, granulated sugar, lemon rind, and salt together in a large saucepan. Cook and stir over moderate heat until the mixture comes to a boil and the butter melts. Remove the pan from heat. Add the flour all at once and stir vigorously.

Return the pan to the burner and continue to stir over moderate heat until the mixture forms a ball and comes away from the sides of the pan. Cook a few minutes longer, until you hear a slight crackling or frying sound. Remove the pan from the heat and cool slightly.

Add the eggs, one at a time. Blend each egg thoroughly into the mixture before adding the next one. Continue stirring until the dough is smooth and thoroughly blended. Add vanilla. Cover the dough and let stand 15–20 minutes.

Preheat oven to 400 degrees. Drop dough by heaping tablespoonfuls on a greased cookie sheet, leaving 2 inches between the puffs. Bake 20–25 minutes, or until the puffs are golden brown. Remove them from the oven to cool on racks.

For the filling: Mix together the ricotta, confectioner's sugar, vanilla, cinnamon, chocolate chips, and pistachios. It's best to fill the cream puffs just before serving: Cut each cream puff horizontally partway through the middle and fill with the chilled ricotta mixture. Sprinkle with confectioners' sugar. Yield: about 20 cream puffs.

(Adapted from *A Continual Feast* by Evelyn Birge Vitz, Ignatius Press, 1985.)

April

Easter

Easter and nature in springtime are rich with Christian symbolism. All around us are signs of the world coming back to life from the dead of winter, just as Christ triumphed over death and sin for our sake. Perhaps because we raise chickens, I'm particularly fond of the egg as an Easter symbol of the new life we find in Christ. Brightly colored, store-bought dyes are dramatic in their own way, but I'm partial to the more muted pastel tones you can achieve when you dye eggs with natural ingredients you might find in your kitchen or garden. Once you learn a few basics, you can get creative and experiment with any number of natural products to produce your own original colors.

Basic Directions for Natural Egg Dyeing

1. Place the eggs in a single layer in a large pan and fill the pan with non-chlorinated water until the eggs are just covered. Eggs take on the color better and are less likely to break if they are not stacked on top of each other

2. Add 1–2 teaspoons of vinegar. Although not necessary, you may also want to add ½ teaspoon alum (available at grocery and drugstores) to make the colors brighter.

3. Add the natural dye material (see below for suggestions according to color). The more natural dye

material you use, the more intense the color will be.

4. Bring the water to a boil. Reduce heat and simmer for 15 minutes.

5. Check the color. If you are pleased with the results, remove eggs from the dye. If you want more intense color, let eggs remain in the dye for a while longer—even overnight in the refrigerator.

To Make	Try Using
Light yellow	Lemon peelings; orange peelings; or ground cumin
Golden yellow	Ground tumeric (find in the spice aisle)
Red or Pink	Fresh or canned beets; fresh, canned, or frozen cherries; crushed whole cranberries (not cranberry sauce); red onion skins; fresh or frozen raspberries
Light green	Fresh or frozen spinach
Blue	Red cabbage leaves; fresh, frozen, or canned blueberries or blackberries
Purple	Grape juice; violet blossoms
Orange	Yellow onion skins (omit vinegar); paprika
Greenish yellow	Yellow Delicious apple peelings; carrot tops
Brown	Strong coffee; black walnut shells

MAY

Mary's Month

May is traditionally a month devoted to Mother Mary. It also just so happens to be the perfect time for planting a garden. A wonderful way to bring together devotion to Mary and the thrill of the great outdoors is to involve the children in planting a Mary garden. Did you know that a number of springtime flowers and herbs are named in honor of Our Lady? Choose some of the following and talk about ways in which each is symbolic of Mary as you plant them with your children. Here's a list to get you started:

Rose:	Like Mary, the rose is known for its beauty and perfection. Among Mary's titles are "First Rose of the Martyrs" and "Soothing Rose of the Afflicted."
Lily:	The white lily is a traditional symbol of purity.
Marigold:	This flower gets its name from "Mary's gold," as marigolds were traditionally planted around shrines to Our Lady in order to surround her with pieces of "gold."
Violet:	Small and sweet, the violet is a long-time symbol of humility.

Snowdrop: This tiny white flower is another symbol of purity.

Juniper bush: There is an old legend that tells of a juniper bush that sprang up to shelter and hide the Holy Family from Herod's men during their flight to Egypt.

Lavender: According to legend, this herb gained its sweet smell from the times when Mary laid the infant Jesus' laundered clothing on lavender bushes to dry.

Lily of the Valley: It is said that these small flowers were formed from Mary's tears as she stood at the cross.

Additionally, a variety of flowers are customarily referred to in terms of belonging to the Virgin Mary. Among these are strawberries, which are considered "our Lady's fruit"; honeysuckle, called "our Lady's fingers"; impatiens, referred to as "Mary's earrings"; foxglove, considered "Mary's gloves"; and lady's slippers are (of course!) "Mary's slippers."

JUNE

Month of June Dedicated to Sacred Heart of Jesus

Friday following Corpus Christi:
Feast of the Sacred Heart of Jesus

June provides parents with a wonderful opportunity to introduce children to the Sacred Heart of Jesus. In my experience, even very young children are impressed by the image of the Sacred Heart with its thorns and fire. During this month, you might make a point of showing your children a statue or prayer card of the Sacred Heart of Jesus and talk about the burning, all-enduring love our Lord has for each of us in his Sacred Heart.

You and your family might also learn a new prayer to the Sacred Heart of Jesus in order to add it to grace or other prayers during this month. One very simple traditional one is: "Sacred Heart of Jesus, I place my trust in thee!"

One of the nicest things about celebrating the feast of the Sacred Heart is that you can adapt any number of secular, heart-themed Valentine's crafts into "Sacred Heart" projects. To get you started, here is an inexpensive, quick, and easy craft that kids of all ages can make as Sacred Heart gifts for friends and family:

Sacred Heart Pencil Toppers

You'll need scissors, colored craft foam, permanent markers, pipe cleaners, and pencils.

Cut a 1–2-inch heart shape from colored craft foam. Using a permanent marker, write a short Sacred Heart message on the front and back. Try something like "Sacred Heart of Jesus" on one side with "Pray for Us" on the other. Next, poke an inch of the pipe cleaner through the bottom of the heart, bend it down, and twist it back around the remaining length of pipe cleaner. Then coil the pipe cleaner tightly around the pencil. Gently pull up on the foam heart so that part of the coil bobbles and moves freely above the pencil, with several loops wrapped around the eraser end.

JULY

July 26: Feast of Saints Ann and Joachim, Grandparents of Jesus

Because Saints. Ann and Joachim were Jesus' grandparents, their feast day provides us with an ideal opportunity to recognize and honor the importance of grandparents in our own families. If your children's grandparents live nearby, this is a wonderful day to visit them, bringing homemade cards or other goodies. For faraway grandparents, mail cards ahead of time, send e-mails, or make phone calls on this special day.

To further help small children understand and appreciate the role of grandparents and their own relationships with extended family members, a nice craft project to try is constructing a miniature family tree:

Family Tree Craft

You'll need a small twig with many branches, green construction paper, crayons or markers, scissors, yarn, a hole punch, a Styrofoam or paper cup, a lump of play dough or other clay, and a glue stick.

Put a lump of clay in the bottom of a paper or Styrofoam cup. Insert the twig securely so that it remains upright.

Cut out big leaves from the green construction paper. Each leaf will represent a person in the child's family and should be big enough to write that person's name on the leaf. Cut at least enough leaves for each of the child's siblings, parents, and grandparents. Then write the names of family members on the leaves, identifying each person's relationship to them as well. For example, on a grandfather's leaf, you might write: "Grandpa: Joe Smith." On a sister's leaf you might write: "Sister: Mary Smith." Use the hole punch to punch a hole on the end of each leaf.

Using the yarn, tie the leaves to branches of the tree. If the twig's shape allows, you might try separating the leaves according to generation within the family: The child's own generation goes at the top of the tree, the parents at the second level, and the grandparents at the bottom. For pre-reading children, you might prefer to glue computer-printed paper photos of family members in place of written names on the leaves.

August

August 15: Feast of the Assumption
of the Blessed Virgin Mary

There is an ancient tradition in parts of Europe in which Catholics bring fresh fruits and herbs to church with them on the feast of the Assumption in order to have them blessed by their parish priests. This blessing of fruits and herbs is meant to remind us of Mary's own fruitfulness and the fact that she was the first of God's children to be "harvested," body and soul, into heaven.

Your parish may not offer a blessing of this kind, but you can bring a bouquet of fresh herbs or a basket of fresh fruit along with you to Mass and ask your priest to bless them afterwards. And there are countless delicious recipes calling for fresh herbs that you can serve up for a special Assumption Day meal. Here are two of our personal favorites that might whet your appetite:

Pesto Chicken

1 tablespoon extra-virgin olive oil

4 skinless, boneless chicken breast halves, cut into strips

4 large cloves of garlic, sliced

3 ½ tablespoons sherry

¼ cup pine nuts

½ cup chopped fresh basil

1 (8-ounce) container sour cream

3 tablespoons grated parmesan cheese
Ground black pepper to taste

Heat the olive oil in a heavy skillet over moderate heat. Add the chicken and cook and stir for about 5 minutes, until lightly browned. Add the garlic and sherry to the skillet; continue to cook and stir until all the liquid has been reduced and the chicken is no longer pink in the middle. Add the pine nuts to the skillet, and cook 2–3 minutes more over moderate heat. Reduce the heat to low, and add the basil, sour cream, parmesan cheese, and pepper to the skillet. Continue cooking until heated through. Serve over rice or pasta.

Fried Sage Leaves

At least 2 dozen large sage leaves, washed and patted dry
Olive oil
Coarse salt

In a heavy skillet, heat about 1 inch of olive oil over medium heat. Add a few of the sage leaves at a time to the hot oil and fry just until they begin to shrivel. Remove the fried leaves from the pan and drain them on a paper towel. Place leaves on a serving plate and sprinkle with coarse salt. That's all there is to it!

September

September 29: Feast of the Archangels
Michael, Gabriel, Raphael

Children love to learn about the angels. If you haven't yet introduced them to the spectacular story of God's creation of the angels, Lucifer's rebellion, the dramatic battle, and St. Michael's thrusting of Satan into hell, this is just the time to do so. A great resource for teaching small children about the angels is a tiny paperback available at most Catholic bookstores: *The Angels: God's Messengers and Our Helpers,* by Father Lawrence Lovasik, SVD. St. Michael is an all-time favorite—especially with young boys—but you might also read some passages from the Bible that mention Gabriel and Raphael in order to familiarize your children with these archangels as well.

Of course, once you've learned about the angels, your family will need a feast day treat. It's tradition at our house to bake angel food cake to celebrate the feast of the archangels. To further dramatize the story of the angels and the great battle, and since you can never have too much cake, you might want to bake up a devil's food cake as well!

Angel Food Cake

1 cup cake flour

1 ½ cups white sugar

12 egg whites

1 ½ teaspoons vanilla extract

1 ½ teaspoons cream of tartar

½ teaspoon salt

Preheat the oven to 375 degrees. Use a 10-inch tube pan that is clean and dry (any amount of oil or residue could deflate the egg whites). Mix and toss together the flour with half the sugar (¾ cup); set this mixture aside.

In a large bowl, beat the egg whites with the vanilla, cream of tartar, and salt, until they form medium stiff peaks. Then add the remaining sugar a little at a time while continuing to beat until stiff peaks form. When the egg white mixture has reached its maximum volume, fold in the flour mixture gradually, one third at a time. Take care not to over-mix. Pour the batter into the tube pan.

Bake the cake for 40–45 minutes in the preheated oven, or until it springs back when touched. Balance the tube pan upside down on the top of a bottle or a funnel to prevent it from decompressing while it cools. When the cake is completely cooled, run a knife around the edge of the tube pan and invert the cake onto a serving plate.

Devil's Food Cake

½ cup butter

3 (1-ounce) squares unsweetened chocolate

2 cups white sugar

2 eggs

1 cup boiled water, slightly cooled

2 ¼ cups all-purpose flour

1 ½ teaspoons baking soda

¼ teaspoon salt

¼ cup milk

1 teaspoon distilled white vinegar

Preheat oven to 350 degrees. Grease and flour a 9 x 13-inch glass or metal baking pan.

In a small saucepan, melt the butter and the unsweetened chocolate. Set aside to cool while you cream together the sugar and the eggs. When the mixture is light in color, add the melted chocolate mixture to the eggs and beat well. Add 1 cup boiled water (still warm) and blend well. At this point, the mixture will be very liquid.

In a separate bowl, stir together the flour, baking soda, and salt. Add this mixture to the chocolate mixture and blend well. Stir together the vinegar and the milk and add to the chocolate batter. Pour batter into prepared pan and bake for about 30 minutes or until a toothpick inserted in the center comes out clean. Cool cake and frost as desired.

OCTOBER

October 4: Feast of St. Francis

Most of us are familiar with this popular saint and founder of the Franciscan Order. He is especially known and beloved for his closeness to the natural world and love for all of God's creation. Popular tales from his life story include the good friar preaching to the birds and taming a wolf that was terrorizing a village. You'll find a wonderful version of this great saint's life story in Tomie De Paola's beautifully illustrated *Francis: The Poor Man of Assisi.*

On St. Francis's feast day, some parishes offer a special Mass with a blessing of the pets afterwards. Even without a special pet blessing, you can lead your children in prayer thanking God for the many blessings of his creation, and in particular for any pets that are part of your family. And of course you'll want to bake a special treat for some lucky dog in your life. Even if you don't have a pet dog, surely you and your children know a deserving one:

Doggie Biscuits

2 ¼ cups whole-wheat flour

½ cup powdered milk

½ teaspoon salt

6 tablespoons butter or shortening

1 egg, beaten

1 tablespoon brown sugar

½ cup cold water

Preheat oven to 350 degrees. Mix flour, powdered milk, and sugar. Cut in shortening until mixture looks like cornmeal. Add egg. Add water. Mix

with a fork until mixture forms a ball. Pat out to
½-inch thickness on a greased cookie sheet. Use
cookie cutters to cut out desired shapes. Bake
25–30 minutes. Woof!

NOVEMBER

Last Sunday of Ordinary Time:
Feast of Christ the King

The feast of Christ the King presents Catholics with
an opportunity to remind themselves that the Catholic
Church is not a democracy. Jesus Christ, our Lord and our
God, is not only the Messiah but also the mighty and
powerful *King* of heaven and earth. We owe him worship,
honor, and respect. After talking with your children a bit
about the feast day and Jesus Christ as our King, you can
lead them in a simple prayer to Christ the King. Then,
you can reinforce the concept of royalty with this fun and
simple craft:

Christ's Crown

You will need plain paper plates; colored construction or tissue paper; paint, markers, or crayons;
scissors; glue; and foil stickers or other crown "dec-
orations."

Cut four crisscrossing slits through the center of
each plate, leaving an inch of space at the edges.
Bend the eight triangles formed by the slits upward,
forming points on the "crown." Paint or color the

crown as desired and then decorate it, using the paper, paints, stickers, ribbons, or even small plastic beads or faux jewels (available at craft supply stores).

DECEMBER

December 6: Feast of St. Nicholas

Good old St. Nicholas—he's the perfect remedy for the "gimmies" many children are prone to during the holy season of Advent. Whether you teach your children to believe in Santa Claus or not, you should be sure to introduce them to St. Nicholas. This great saint, the real-life bishop on whom the modern-day character of Santa Claus is based, was well-known for his kindness to children, his concern for the poor, and his generous acts of charity. Teaching children about this man's holy life and challenging them to imitate him are wonderful ways to minimize materialism and emphasize giving to others at this time of year.

There are so many beautiful children's picture books that tell the story of St. Nicholas that I cannot choose just one to recommend. I do recommend, however, that you make good use of your local library and check out a few of the titles that are available. After reading the stories, there are any number of traditional St. Nicholas games, recipes, and crafts from around the world that families can enjoy together. The very best resource for all of these is an amazing website that we return to every year: www.stnicholascenter.org.

Here's just one to get you started:

St. Nicholas Pfeffernuesse
(German Pepper Cookies)

3 eggs

2 cups brown sugar

2 cups all-purpose flour

½ teaspoon baking powder

½ teaspoon baking soda

¼ teaspoon salt

½ teaspoon ground cloves

½ teaspoon allspice

¼ teaspoon nutmeg

½ teaspoon ground black pepper

1 tablespoon cinnamon

1 cup walnuts, chopped

1 pound seedless raisins

½ cup citron, chopped

confectioners' sugar

Preheat oven to 375 degrees. Use an electric mixer to beat eggs until they are light. Add the brown sugar a little at a time and beat well after each addition. In a separate bowl, mix together the flour, baking powder, baking soda, salt, spices, and pepper. Stir in the nuts, raisins, and citron. Add the

dry ingredients to the eggs and sugar mixture and
stir to make stiff dough. Shape into 1-inch balls and
roll until smooth. Bake cookies on greased baking
sheets for 10 minutes. Remove cookies from the
oven and roll them in confectioners' sugar while
they are still warm. Once cooled, store in an airtight
container. Makes about 5 dozen cookies. (Adapted
from www.stnicholascenter.org.)

*Dear Lord, I know that I am responsible for passing
on the gift of my Catholic faith to my children. I am
honored by this responsibility, but frightened by it also. I
need your help. Show me how to make our faith a real
part of our family life. Help me to teach my children that
we aren't just Catholic on Sunday, but every day, all the
time. Bless our home as we celebrate special days here
together. Inspire in our hearts a desire to follow the holy
examples of your saints and help us to gain the graces
that are found in observing Church traditions. Through
our shared activities, draw us closer to you and to one
another. Help us to grow in holiness and faith here in the
domestic church of our home. Amen.*

six

Can I Really Have a Spiritual Life While Caring for All These Little People?

Doing It All

Good news, ladies. You can have it all. You can be it all. And you can do it all. If you don't believe me, just take a look at the covers of the popular women's magazines in the checkout aisle of your local supermarket. There you'll find articles detailing exactly how you can (and should!) be the world's best wife, mother, lover, career woman, homemaker, political activist, and Brownie troop leader...all without breaking a sweat. Or a perfectly manicured fingernail, for that matter.

I know this is an issue that speaks to the hearts of women everywhere because it's a question I get asked all the time: You have a husband, children, work, a house, a spiritual life, *and* homeschooling. How do you do it all?

How do *I* do it all? That's actually an easy question to answer: I don't. Nobody can and nobody does.

While it's true that today's women have more options and opportunities than those of past generations, our modern culture's insistence that women can have and do it *all* sometimes leaves us feeling like failures when we don't and we can't. And yet, stubbornly, we cling to the notion that some women do indeed have and do it all, don't we?

The fact is, however, that the most any of us can do is "the best we can" with what we are given—our individual abilities and circumstances. It can be exceedingly difficult, however, to find balance between a seemingly endless multitude of responsibilities and our own needs. Well, since there is no magic formula for "doing it all," and the demands for our time and energy aren't going anywhere, I figure that we might as well come up with a plan for keeping our lives in check.

Finding Balance

The simplest formula for balance, success, and happiness I have found goes like this: Put God at the center of your life, recognize your duties and priorities, and then set up your day-to-day activities in accordance with those. A particularly helpful book for helping Catholic women do this in an organized fashion is *A Mother's Rule of Life* by Holly Pierlot (see the Resource Guide on page 151). But there are other ways as well.

First and foremost, I think it's important for mothers, especially those with young children, to recognize that they have been called to an active life and an active vocation, not a contemplative one. This means that while spiritual meditation, daily Mass, and lengthy Scripture studies are noble and worthy pursuits, they are not necessarily the particular ways in which God is calling you to a closer relationship with him during this stage in your life.

What God wants most from anyone at any stage in life is cheerful obedience to his will. The fact that a young family requires your near-constant attention is a pretty clear indication of God's will for the ways in which you should spend your days. I once resolved to do some kind of spiritual reading every day. On the very first day, however, when I sat down with my copy of *Holiness for Housewives* by Hubert Van Zeller (see the Resource Guide, page 151), my two-year-old son took advantage of my distraction by attempting to flush his father's silk tie down the toilet. I figured God was telling me to put down the book.

You know how it goes. When the baby must be changed, the baby *must be changed*. When the five-year-old fights, he needs correction. When the toddler falls, she needs comforting. Right now.

Giving Everything to the Lord

It's important, though, to spend some quiet time in prayer in order to discern God's will and to keep it at the forefront of your mind, even in the midst of chaotic family life. How can a busy mother do that? I have found that my "Morning Offering" can be an enormously help-ful spiritual tool here. You have probably heard of this spiritual practice before, but perhaps your busy life has pulled you away from the habit of praying it daily. Here's a commonly heard one that I like to use:

> O Jesus, through the Immaculate Heart of Mary,
> I offer you all my prayers, works, joys,
>   and sufferings of this day,
> for all the intentions of your Sacred Heart,
> in union with the Holy Sacrifice of the Mass
>   throughout the world,
> in reparation for my sins, for the intentions of
>   all our associates,
> and in particular for the intentions of the Holy Father.
> Amen.

There are lots of different morning offering prayers you can memorize and then recite daily as a means of giving your entire day over to God, no matter how distracted you become. In this way, your entire day—all the way down to the tiniest, most mundane detail—is transformed into a beautiful gift for God.

I sometimes also find it beneficial to repeat my morning offering throughout the day as a way of reminding myself that my work, sacrifices, and obedience—however silly and meaningless they might seem by human standards—have been offered to God.

Do you have to break up yet another biting fight between pre-schoolers? "O Jesus…"

Did the baby dump a giant bowl of spaghetti on her head on a night when you were hoping to skip baths? "O Jesus…"

Were you up all night with a sick child, but the next morning everyone still wants breakfast, the laundry still needs to be done, and schoolwork too? "O Jesus…"

I don't fancy myself a spiritual powerhouse. Using a morning offering is a humble, simple practice, to be sure. But I believe it's an invaluable spiritual tool for distracted, busy mothers. At any given trying moment, when I'm tempted toward self-pity, it alone has the power to switch my focus away from myself and onto God. It yields much greater fruit than all those hours of spiritual reading I never got around to.

Screening Our Influences

A few years ago, I checked a book out of the library about motherhood. I could tell from the back cover that the author was anything but Catholic, but she was a well-known writer and I was familiar with her work on other topics. I thought at the very worst that the book would be an interesting read that would only *not* affirm my Catholic view of my vocation.

I was wrong.

The book made compelling reading. Unfortunately, it was well-written and persuasive in its assertions about the "trap" of motherhood. The author, a mother of two young boys, described a feeling of being "duped" by motherhood. In the beginning, she was charmed by the sweetness and innocence of babyhood and toddlers, but then she had great trouble getting past the onerous responsibility implied by her own parenthood. She resented it. And she especially resented the fact that her husband seemed impervious to the kind of guilt she suffered as she struggled between commitment to motherhood and her own selfish desires for greater wealth and personal freedom. Quite predictably, she blamed her unhappiness on a sexist culture that places unfair burdens on mothers as primary caregivers for their children.

Objectively, I could see the weaknesses in the author's arguments. Intellectually, I knew the truth about the dignity and value of motherhood. And yet, somehow, the poisonous thinking in that piece of writing seeped its way into my psyche. During the days in which I was immersed in that book, my worldview was tainted by the bitterness and resentment within its pages. Suddenly, my son didn't just need a diaper change in the middle of the night—he was oppressing me! My husband didn't just meet up with friends for a weeknight basketball game—he was burdening me with his offspring and selfishly taking me for granted!

We need to be careful about the kinds of outside influences we allow to shape our hearts and minds

In the end, the book didn't permanently damage my relationship with my family, but it did open my eyes to a very important truth: We need to be very careful about the kinds of outside influences we allow to shape our hearts and minds. In this case, the author's misunderstandings and misrepresentations, despite my recognizing them for what they were, still managed to influence my emotions.

It made me think a bit about what other kinds of negative influences I might unthinkingly be exposing myself to. When I thought about it, I realized that I had a few friends or acquaintances whose views of marriage and motherhood were vastly different from mine...and really rather negative. I realized there were certain television shows I watched that had the potential to warp my idea of "normal" family life.

When it comes to negative influences, grown women are not as easily swayed as children are, but we do tend to be emotional creatures. There's nothing wrong with that—it's how God made us, and female emotionalism is the very thing that enables us to love our families so well and with such heartfelt devotion. But the conversations and ideas with which we fill our heads are likely to influence our emotions. And our emotions are likely to influence our thoughts, our attitudes, and ultimately, our actions.

Because God's call to motherhood can be such a personally challenging vocation, it only makes sense to surround ourselves with as much support and encouragement in this endeavor as possible.

I don't mean that we should all stay at home, hide in the hall closet, and avoid anyone who disagrees with us. I do, however, think a happy mother should take care to protect her own emotional well-being. None of us is immune to temptation and it seems only sensible to choose our reading materials, television programs, and friendships carefully. In a world of negativity, every mother should take care to cultivate a cheerful outlook and then to guard her healthy, positive attitude like the priceless treasure it is.

Making More Time for God

It can't get much easier than having other people make excuses for you, can it? Because I have small children, people don't tend to expect too much of me. They are always cutting me slack. Most people I meet seem to think that if I've managed to dress myself and keep the baby's bottom clean for most of the day, I've accomplished something genuinely admirable. And in fact there are some days where I think I deserve a medal for having accomplished exactly that.

But surely not every day. All too often, I've found, I am eager to play along with well-meaning excuse-makers simply because everything is easier if I set the bar very low. Especially when it comes to my spiritual life.

Of course I don't have time for daily prayer, I find myself nodding in agreement. I have all these little kids to care for! And of course I can never make it to weekday Mass—I'm just trying to keep my head above water! Scripture study? Not with my schedule! The Rosary? In your dreams!

But one day not too long ago, I had to ask myself: Is all of that really true? Do I really have no time or energy for these things...or am I just choosing to spend my time and energy on other things?

I endeavored to find out. First, I made up a list of those things—those few basic activities or accomplishments—that I thought I should be doing on a regular basis. Everything from schoolwork, cleaning house, preparing meals, caring for children, exercise, relaxation, and private prayer went on this list. That was the easy part. Though we all have different lists, we all have a pretty good idea of what things we should be doing on a regular basis.

But then came the more painful, eye-opening step: I needed to find out if my list of professed priorities actually matched up with my real-life actions. I spent the next couple of days documenting—actually writing down—every single thing I did. This sounds like a major project, but it's quite simple to do, really. Wear a watch and set the timer to go off every thirty minutes. Every time it beeps, write down what you spent the last thirty minutes doing. And be painfully honest, even if it seems ridiculous. If you actually did spend forty-five minutes breaking up arguments, picking your nails, and blowing raspberries on the baby's belly...write that down. If you actually did spend an hour and a half talking about nothing with your next-door neighbor...write that down. This is your own private list, after all. For it to be useful, you need to be honest.

When you're done, the last step is to compare your two lists. Does the list of things you know you should be doing even come close to your actual doings? If yes, good for you! Carry on! Godspeed!

If not, join the club. And now let's fix it.

All too often, mothers at home tend to feel like victims of their own lives. I know I've felt that way more times than I can count.

All too often, mothers at home tend to feel like victims of their own lives.

"I don't make choices," I complained to a friend one day. "My life just kind of happens to me and then I react to it."

Well, that's not a very intelligent way to live, is it? I found that the making and comparing of my two lists helped me to be more conscious of the choices I was making in my daily life. After all, choosing to live in blissful ignorance of those choices is a choice in itself. One of the most glaring discrepancies I found was in praying the Rosary. I had it high on my list of priorities; it really was something I thought I could reasonably accomplish on a regular basis, either praying it by myself or with the family. But I almost never did.

Why was that? I had to be honest with myself. It wasn't because I never *had* twenty free minutes in my day. Just by looking at my list of daily activities, it was easy to see that I did. I was just *choosing* to do other things with those twenty minutes: watch TV, read a book, browse recipes, or talk on the phone. These aren't bad things, of course, but none of them ranked as highly on my priorities list as praying the Rosary did. Somehow, though, they were coming first.

A change was in order. If I was going to claim that praying the Rosary was a personal priority, I needed to back up that claim with some action. I looked at our daily schooling schedule, found a twenty-minute slot, and cautiously penciled in "Rosary."

Scary, right? Well, for the first few days of breaking the kids in, it was an ordeal. They couldn't find their favorite rosary picture books, they fought over who got to use the pink rosary beads, and they whined that praying just "one decade" would be so much easier. But we did it. And eventually, praying the Rosary during that time slot became a habit and a matter of routine. The kids came to expect it, I planned around it, and most days...we actually did it. No big deal.

My small success with the Rosary opened my eyes to the obvious: Ultimately, I am in control of how I spend my days. I am not a hapless victim of my life and circumstances. It sounds silly, but this was an empowering revelation for me: I can decide which things are most important to me and make them happen on a regular basis. That could mean more time for exercise or daily prayer.

The point is, you choose. Consciously. And in the end, however you choose to spend the twenty-four hours in any given day, you will have the peace of mind and satisfaction of making the conscious decision to do so.

Move Over, Martyr Mom

Thanksgiving happens to be one of my personal favorite holidays. I love the focus on family togetherness, good food, and tradition. On one particular Thanksgiving a couple of years ago, however, our celebration was going to be a bit different; I was going to be the hostess. Instead of going to my parents' house and joining a throng of brothers, sisters, aunts, uncles, and cousins, as Dan and I had done every year since we were first married, we would be staying home. We had invited Dan's father and brother to join us, and the kids were thrilled at the prospect of having special company for a special holiday dinner in our own home.

It was a momentous occasion. And, unfortunately, that morning as I stuffed the turkey, peeled potatoes, and kneaded the dough for dinner rolls, I was in a momentous mood to match. You see, the baby did not know it was Thanksgiving. And even if she knew, she likely wouldn't have cared. She understood only that she was fighting a cold, that her sniffles had prevented her from sleeping much the previous night, and that she wanted to be in her mother's arms. But her mother, stressed by the prospect of hosting a holiday dinner, exhausted from spending the previous night with a feverish, fussy baby, and feeling the scratchy beginnings of a sore throat herself, was not very accommodating.

Dan tried holding her and I coaxed a few of the older kids into attempting to entertain her with books and blocks, but she was having none of it. Sleepy, sickly babies want their mommies. No substitutions, please.

But, since I was determined not to abandon our special Thanksgiving dinner plans, and because pride would not allow me to hand off to a less experienced cook such crucial tasks as shaping the dinner rolls, I held baby Gabby in one arm while I worked the dough with the other. She sniffled while I consulted recipes, chopped carrots, and sliced almonds. I shifted her weight from one hip to the other as I measured, diced, and poured. She leaned her head against my chest and I felt her grow heavier. And heavier. And heavier. Until at last I was convinced she was asleep.

I carried her upstairs and placed her gingerly in her crib, covered her with a blanket, and tiptoed out of the room. Now, delirious with the thrill of having free use of both my arms, I raced downstairs and attacked my house like a mad woman. The kitchen was a disaster of dirty dishes, there were still appetizer platters to prepare, the table wasn't set, and I had hoped to have a minute to tidy up the living room and bathroom before dinner. And— the worst part—I was already feeling exhausted.

I swept the floor. Then the kids came running in from playing outside, tracked mud, and left grubby handprints on every household surface. I loaded breakfast dishes and dirty pans into the dishwasher before I realized it still contained clean dishes from the previous cycle. I checked the roasting turkey and found the pan I had chosen for it was too small to contain its greasy juices. The drippings were spattering the inside of the oven, crackling and smoking.

"What is that smell?" Dan asked, wrinkling up his nose and blinking his eyes in the hazy, smoke-filled kitchen. I answered him with a glare.

When yet another child came running into the kitchen, poured—I mean, spilled—himself a glass of juice from the refrigerator, and asked when Grandpa would be coming, I answered him with a slammed cabinet door.

As the smoky smell of turkey grease filled the house, an angry black cloud settled ominously over my head. I threw some pot lids into the sink and they made a satisfying clang. I could feel my family's eyes on me as I gritted my teeth, ferociously mashed the potatoes, and viciously hacked at a block of frozen peas.

After watching the "show" for several minutes, my heroic husband ventured an offer of help with setting the table. I think I growled at him.

"You know," he finally dared to tell me, "we all would rather have peanut butter sandwiches for Thanksgiving dinner as long as you were happy and not behaving like this."

Ouch.

Here I thought that by cooking up a fantastic feast for Thanksgiving I was being a good wife and mother. The truth was, though, that regardless of how the dinner turned out, I was failing miserably. I thought I had been sacrificing for the good of my family, but really I had subjected them all to a serious case of Martyr Mom.

Perhaps Martyr Mom sometimes makes an appearance in your home. You'll know her if she does. Martyr Mom is stubborn. She takes on too much, refuses help, and makes no concessions, all in the name of doing things the right way and being generous with her family. But, because she is only human after all, Martyr Mom winds up feeling pressured and put out. She scolds, she snaps, she pouts, and she sighs. Quite frankly, Martyr Mom is not a very pleasant person.

Sometimes it's necessary to take care of yourself so that you will be better able to care for others.

She almost always manages to make her family—the very people she presumes to be serving—miserable.

Your family doesn't want that kind of "generosity."

If you've ever flown in an airplane, you already know how to combat Martyr Mom. In case of emergency, the flight attendants remind us, put on your own oxygen mask first. Only then will you be prepared to help others with theirs. In other words, sometimes it's necessary to take care of yourself so that you will be better able to care for others.

When the baby claimed my attention on that Thanksgiving Day, instead of sacrificing my own rest and personal well-being, I should have accepted help and made a few concessions. After spending a wakeful night, I should have reassessed my meal plans and set more reasonable goals for the day. I should have settled for a less-than-sparkling bathroom. I should have let a nine-year-old shape the dough and enjoyed the creative-looking dinner rolls that might have resulted. I should have rocked the baby in a nearby rocking chair while someone else peeled the potatoes. I should have removed a few superfluous items from my to-do list and worked peacefully with the time I had.

On that fateful Thanksgiving, I caught myself a little late, but we still managed to salvage the day. I delegated a few of the remaining dinner preparations and sat down for a bit. When the baby awoke from her nap, we simply sat together and cuddled. Martyr Mom made a hasty departure. A sense of peace and acceptance filled the house.

After Grandpa arrived, when I realized that I had miscalculated the size of the turkey and it would take ninety minutes longer to cook than I had anticipated, I moved the mashed potatoes to a back burner and served up the appetizers. And then I laughed. We all did. Finally, when we all sat down to a smoked turkey and somewhat gummy mashed potato dinner, Dan and the children lavished my efforts with heartfelt compliments. They said it was a wonderful dinner. And, smilingly, I thanked them.

See? Put on your own oxygen mask first. Then everyone breathes easy.

Dear Lord, I am so many things: a wife, a mother, a daughter, a sister, a friend, a neighbor, an employee, and a volunteer. Despite my many labels, help me to remember that I am first and foremost a child of God. Above all else, keep me focused on the unique relationship I have with you. Even when the baby throws up in the car. Even when the dog digs up the neighbor's prize-winning geraniums. Even when a crayon gets run through the dryer. And especially when I am just weary of it all and looking for a break. Help me to see that I will find the "break" I need in you. Turn my heart and mind toward you often throughout my busy day. Remind me that my cheerful acceptance of little sacrifices and distractions can add up to a priceless gift of love, if only I will give them to you. Amen.

Resource Guide for Catholic Families

BOOKS

For Women/Mothers:

Guarendi, Ray. *Discipline that Lasts a Lifetime: The Best Gift You Can Give Your Kids*. Ann Arbor, MI: Charis Books, 2003.
> *Practical parenting advice from a clinical psychologist and father of ten children.*

Kineke, Genevieve. *The Authentic Catholic Woman*. Cincinnati: Servant Publications, 2006.
> *Offers a spiritual and practical outline to help all women understand God's plan for their lives.*

Pierlot, Holly. *A Mother's Rule of Life*. Manchester, NH: Sophia Institute Press, 2004.
> *How to bring order to your home and peace to your soul.*

Santorum, Karen. *Everyday Graces: A Child's Book of Good Manners*. Wilmington, DE: Intercollegiate Studies Institute, 2003.
> *A basic book of manners for Catholic children.*

Van Zeller, Hubert. *Holiness for Housewives (and Other Working Women)*. Manchester, NH: Sophia Institute Press, 1997.
> *Finding God among the dishes and diapers.*

Vitz, Evelyn Birge. *A Continual Feast*. New York: Harper & Row, 1985.
> *A cookbook to celebrate the joys of faith and family throughout the Christian year.*

Welborn, Amy. *A Catholic Woman's Book of Days*. Chicago: Loyola Press, 2005.

> *A daily Scripture reading and mini-meditation for busy Catholic women.*

For Education:

Berquist, Laura. *Designing Your Own Classical Curriculum: A Guide to Catholic Home Education*. 3rd ed. Ignatius Press, 1998.

> *A comprehensive, basic guide for designing your own Catholic homeschool curriculum.*

Foss, Elizabeth. *Real Learning: Education in the Heart of the Home*. St. Paul, MN: By Way of the Family Press, 2003.

> *A lovely, practical guide to Catholic homeschooling for real mothers and real families.*

Gibson, Cay. *Catholic Mosaic: Living the Liturgical Year with Literature*. Lake Ariel, PA: Hillside Education, 2006.

> *Living out the liturgical year through children's literature and craft projects.*

For Marriage:

Hahn, Kimberly. *Life-Giving Love: Embracing God's Beautiful Design for Marriage*. Ann Arbor, MI: Charis Books, 2002.

> *God's wonderful plan for the family is clearly revealed in the time-tested teachings of the Catholic Church.*

Hajduk, David. *God's Plan for You: Life, Love, Marriage, and Sex*. Boston: Pauline Books & Media, 2006.

> *A book that makes John Paul II's magnificent vision of the human person accessible to today's youth.*

John Paul II. Translated and introduced by Michael M. Waldstein. *Man and Woman He Created Them: A Theology of the Body*. Boston: Pauline Books & Media, 2006.

> *In this new critical translation, John Paul II's magnificent vision of the human person is presented with meticulous scholarship and profound insight.*

Kippley, John. *Marriage Is for Keeps: Foundations for Christian Marriage*. Cincinnati: Foundation for the Family, 1993.

> *Helpful thoughts and information for engaged and married couples alike.*

Paul VI. *Humanae Vitae (Of Human Life)*. Boston: Pauline Books & Media, 1968.

Percy, Anthony. *Theology of the Body Made Simple: Discover John Paul II's radical teaching on sex, love, and the meaning of life*. Boston: Pauline Books & Media, 2006.

> *A simple introduction to the basic premise of Theology of the Body.*

Second Vatican Council. *Gaudium et Spes (Pastoral Constitution on the Church in the Modern World)*. Boston: Pauline Books & Media, 1965.

West, Christopher. *Theology of the Body for Beginners*. West Chester, PA: Ascension Press, 2004.

> *An introduction to Pope John Paul II's teachings on human sexuality.*

WEB SITES
For Women/Mothers:

Catholic Mom Community: www.cmomc.org.
> *Message boards designed to provide faithful support for every kind of Catholic mother.*

Catholic Moms: www.catholicmom.com.
> *Crafts, articles, information, and inspiration.*

Domestic Church: www.domestic-church.com.
> *Essays, Catholic teaching, family projects.*

Elizabeth Ministry: www.elizabethministry.com.
> *Christian support for the joys, challenges, and sorrows of the childbearing years.*

La Leche League: www.lalecheleague.org.
> *For breastfeeding information and encouragement.*

For Education:

Catholic Heritage Curricula: www.chcweb.com.
> *Books, curricula, and family resources for Catholic education.*

Emmanuel Books: www.emmanuelbooks.com.
> *Books for catechism, homeschooling, and Catholic family living.*

Love 2 Learn: www.love2learn.net.
> *Favorite resource and reviews for Catholic homeschoolers.*

St. Nicholas Center: www.stnicholascenter.org.
> *Stories, books, games, crafts, and recipes for celebrating St. Nicholas.*

For News and Information:

Catholic Answers: www.catholic.com.
> *Thorough, faithful explanations of Catholic teaching.*

Catholic Exchange: www.catholicexchange.com.
> *News, interviews, forums, and articles, updated daily.*

EWTN: www.ewtn.com.
> *Catholic news and information.*

For Marriage:

Couple to Couple League: www.ccli.org.
> *Natural Family Planning resources and education.*

One More Soul: www.omsoul.com.
> *Pro-life resources for married couples and resources supporting teen abstinence.*

Pope Paul VI Institute: www.popepaulvi.com.
> *Building a culture of life in women's health.*

Newspapers/Magazines

Catholic Mother Magazine, www.catholicmother.ca or 14127 60A
    Avenue, Surrey, B.C. V3X 1C3 Canada.
       Inspiration for Catholic moms.

Faith & Family, www.faithandfamilymag.com, phone: 1-800-356-
    9916.
       The magazine of Catholic living.

Magnificat, www.magnificat.net, phone: 1-866-273-5215.
       *Daily prayers and meditations from the Mass and Liturgy of
       the Hours.*

The National Catholic Register, www.ncregister.com, phone:
    1-800-421-3230.
       *A weekly newspaper for active Catholics, at the service of
       families.*

DANIELLE BEAN is Senior Editor of *Faith & Family* magazine and author of *My Cup of Tea: Musings of a Catholic Mom* (Pauline Books & Media, 2005). She and her husband, Dan, live in New Hampshire, where they homeschool their eight children. It is in her primary vocation, marriage and motherhood, that Danielle finds the source of inspiration for all her writing. To read more of her work, visit www.DanielleBean.com.

Moms everywhere are drinking in the
humor, wisdom, and spiritual refreshment of
Danielle Bean's first book, My Cup of Tea!

"Danielle writes about the everyday occurrences in the life of a
Catholic mom with a voice that will sound familiar to you—
it's your voice, my voice, the voice of my mom...the voice of all
of us who are working diligently to love and raise our children
to be wonderful individuals who know and love their faith."

— Catholic Online

"Bean is a talented wordsmith who manages to give a powerful
witness to the joy of having a large family. Her writing touch-
es a universal chord and avoids the judgmental attitude that
can plague those living a Catholic life against the grain of the
popular culture."

— National Catholic Register

"In her essays, Bean is conscious of God's superintending prov-
idence...she manages to draw universal lessons from personal
experience without ever being preachy. Her captivating style
makes these edifying reflections a pleasure to read."

— First Things

My Cup of Tea:
Musings of a Catholic Mom
ISBN: 0-8198-4837-9
PRICE: $15.95

www.pauline.org
1-800-876-4463

BOOKS & MEDIA

The Daughters of St. Paul operate book and media centers at the following addresses. Visit, call or write the one nearest you today, or find us on the World Wide Web, www.pauline.org

CALIFORNIA
3908 Sepulveda Blvd, Culver City, CA 90230	310-397-8676
2640 Broadway Street, Redwood City, CA 94063	650-369-4230
5945 Balboa Avenue, San Diego, CA 92111	858-565-9181

FLORIDA
145 S.W. 107th Avenue, Miami, FL 33174	305-559-6715

HAWAII
1143 Bishop Street, Honolulu, HI 96813	808-521-2731
Neighbor Islands call:	866-521-2731

ILLINOIS
172 North Michigan Avenue, Chica□go, IL 60601	312-346-4228

LOUISIANA
4403 Veterans Memorial Blvd, Metairie, LA 70006	504-887-7631

MASSACHUSETTS
885 Providence Hwy, Dedham, MA 02026	781-326-5385

MISSOURI
9804 Watson Road, St. Louis, MO 63126	314-965-3512

NEW JERSEY
561 U.S. Route 1, Wick Plaza, Edison, NJ 08817	732-572-1200

NEW YORK
150 East 52nd Street, New York, NY 10022	212-754-1110

PENNSYLVANIA
9171-A Roosevelt Blvd, Philadelphia, PA 19114	215-676-9494

SOUTH CAROLINA
243 King Street, Charleston, SC 29401	843-577-0175

TENNESSEE
4811 Poplar Avenue, Memphis, TN 38117	901-761-2987

TEXAS
114 Main Plaza, San Antonio, TX 78205	210-224-8101

VIRGINIA
1025 King Street, Alexandria, VA 22314	703-549-3806

CANADA
3022 Dufferin Street, Toronto, ON M6B 3T5	416-781-9131

¡También somos su fuente para libros, videos y música en español!